THOMAS MERTON, MONK

EDITED BY BROTHER PATRICK HART

thomas merton, monk

a monastic tribute

IMAGE BOOKS

A DIVISION OF DOUBLEDAY & COMPANY, INC.
GARDEN CITY, NEW YORK
1976

Image Books edition published by special arrangement with Sheed and Ward, Inc.

Image Books edition February 1976

Cum Permissu Superiorum

ISBN: 0-385-11244-0

Copyright © 1974 by The Abbey of Gethsemani
Printed in the United States of America

To the Memory of

THOMAS MERTON

1915 – 1968

He walked with God
and was seen no more
because God took him.

Genesis V:24

ACKNOWLEDGMENTS

Grateful acknowledgment is made to the authors, editors, and publishers of the following journals in which some of these essays first appeared, although in considerably different form: *The American Benedictine Review, Cistercian Studies, Continuum, The Lamp, Lumen Vitae, Monastic Exchange, Monastic Studies*. The article by Father Jean Leclercq was written originally as an introduction to Thomas Merton's posthumous volume, *Contemplation in a World of Action*, and is reprinted here in a revised version with permission of the author and the publisher, Doubleday & Company, Inc., New York. "Firebird" and "Out of a Cloud," two poems by Sister Thérèse Lentfoehr, first appeared in *America* magazine (copyright by America Press) and are published here with the authorization of the poet and the editor. The cover portrait of Thomas Merton by Victor Hammer is reproduced with the permission of Mrs. Victor Hammer of Lexington, Kentucky, and Mr. Edgar Kaufmann, Jr., New York, in whose private collection the original portrait remained until April 1975 when it was destroyed by fire.

Contents

The articles and poems chosen for this volume were written by monks and nuns from Europe and America, most of whom knew Father Louis ('Thomas Merton) personally. They bear witness to Merton's contemplative vision, and reflect the monastic frame of reference for his influence as a spiritual force in the fifties and as a social critic and bridge-builder between East and West in the sixties. We wish to thank all those who have so generously cooperated in the preparation of this book dedicated to the memory of Thomas Merton, in commemoration of the fifth anniversary of his passage through death to life. It is a sincere gesture of our gratitude to God for the great gift He has given us, and to Father Louis for sharing so much of himself with us during his twenty-seven years as a Cistercian monk. We trust it will be received and read by others in the same spirit.

At the inauguration of the Merton Studies Center at Bellarmine College (Louisville, Kentucky) on November 10, 1963, Father Merton summarized the unifying element in his writings in the following terms: "Whatever I may have written, I think it can all be reduced in the end to this one root truth: that God calls human persons to union with Himself and with one another in Christ, in the Church, which is His Mystical Body. It is also a witness to the fact that there is, and must be, in the Church, a contemplative life which has no other function than to realize these mysterious things, and return to God all the thanks and praise that human hearts can give Him" (*The Thomas Merton Studies Center*, Unicorn Press, Santa Barbara, 1971, pp. 14–15).

During the five years since Thomas Merton's death, a number of eulogies have been published, and also more serious studies on the monk, his life, and concerns, in an effort to evaluate his contribution to our age. At least twenty-five doctoral candidates from all over the world have chosen Merton or some aspect of his writings or thought as the subject of their research. Each has shed light on his rich and complex personality.

However, it seems to some who knew him well in religious life, that the fruitfulness of his work was a result not only of his great natural gifts of expression and communication, but above all of his total dedication to his contemplative commitment as a monk.

Abbot John Eudes Bamberger has written elsewhere: "Whatever may be said about Merton, if it will be said truly, it must present his vision and his work as the fruit of the knowledge of God bought with a faith come alive through contemplation" (preface to *Pray to Live*, by Henri Nouwen, Fides, Notre Dame, 1972). And as Father Jean Leclercq expressed it so well in these pages: "at the heart of everything he said was his vocation, his monastic experience. He saw everything through a monk's eyes."

Merton often wrote of the deliberate irrelevance of the monk in society. A few weeks before his death, in speaking to men and women of all the religious traditions of the East and West, he concerned himself again with the theme of the basic irrelevance of the monk, the marginal man, as manifested above all in the fact of death. "He struggles with the fact of death, trying to seek something deeper than death, and the office of the monk, or the marginal person, the meditative person or the poet, is to go beyond death even in this life, to go beyond the dichotomy of life and death and to be, therefore, a witness to life" (*The Asian Journal of Thomas Merton*).

For the monk, *being* must come before, and is more important than, *doing*, and as for any Christian, love and faith must take precedence over works. Thomas Merton often emphasized that the monk is not defined by his task or by his usefulness to society. In the opening chapter of *Contemplation in a World of Action*, Merton spells out the useless character of the monk: "In a certain sense he is supposed to be 'useless' because his mission is not to *do* this or that job but to *be* a man of God. He does not live in order to exercise a specific function: his business is life itself. This means that monasticism aims at the cultivation of a certain *quality* of life, a level of awareness, a depth of consciousness, an area of transcendence and of adoration which are not usually possible in an active secular existence."

Father Merton was fully aware of the dangers of pure activism both within the monastery and outside it which stressed doing to the detriment of being (and becoming). The following warning should suffice to bear out his convictions: "He who attempts to act and do for others or for the world without deepening his own self-understanding, freedom, integrity and capacity to love, will not have anything to give others. He will communicate to them nothing but the contagion of his own obsessions, his aggressivity, his egocentered ambitions, his delusions about ends and means" (p. 5).

What then is the relationship of the contemplative to the Church and to the world for Thomas Merton? He certainly objected to the idea of a total rejection of the world, a turning one's back on the world in disdain. He expressed it very well in his "Author's Note" at the beginning of *Seeds of Destruction:* "The monastic flight from the world into the desert is not a mere refusal to know anything about the world, but a total rejection of all standards of judgment which imply attachment to a history of delusion, egoism and sin. Not of course a vain denial that the monk too is a sinner (this would be an even worse delusion), but a definitive refusal to participate in those activities which have no other fruit than to prolong the reign of untruth, greed, cruelty and arrogance in the world of men."

Merton felt the contemplative must share with others something of his life of prayer, as well as a deep concern and compassion for modern man in his anguish and suffering. Nevertheless, he was convinced that "our greatest and most unique service to the Church is precisely our life of contemplation itself. Our silence and solitude are not mere luxuries and privileges which we have acquired at the Church's expense: they are necessary gifts of God to the Church in and through us. They are part of the precious inheritance of

Christian truth and experience which God has confided to us to hold in trust, in order that the spirit of prayer and contemplation may continue to exist in the whole Church and in the world of our time" (*Contemplation in a World of Action*, p. 182).

Yet this did not come from any triumphalistic notion of the contemplative life, as can be seen from this moving passage from Father Merton's response to an invitation to say something by way of a message of the contemplative to the world: "O my brother, the contemplative is not the man who has fiery visions of the cherubim carrying God on their imagined chariot, but simply he who has risked his mind in the desert beyond language and beyond ideas where God is encountered in the nakedness of pure trust; that is to say, in the surrender of our own poverty and incompleteness in order no longer to clench our minds in a cramp upon themselves, as if thinking made us exist. The message of hope the contemplative offers you, then, brother, is not that you need to find your way through the jungle of language and problems that today surround God: but that whether you understand or not, God loves you, is present to you, lives in you, dwells in you, calls you, saves you, and offers you an understanding and light which are like nothing you ever found in books or heard in sermons. The contemplative has nothing to tell you except to reassure you and say that if you dare to penetrate your own heart, and risk the sharing of that solitude with the lonely other who seeks God through you and with you, then you will truly recover the light and the capacity to understand what is beyond words and beyond explanations because it is too close to be explained: it is the intimate union in the depths of your own heart, of God's spirit and your own secret inmost self, so that you and He are in all truth One Spirit. I love you, in Christ" (for complete text see "As Man to Man," *Cistercian Studies*, IV: 1, 1969).

BROTHER PATRICK HART
Abbey of Gethsemani
10 December 1973

Before dawn on a cool September morning in 1968 three of us trod our way through the wet grass up past the old sheep barn, stopping long enough to catch our breath at the top of the hill leading into the thick woods. As we crossed the fence gate we caught sight of the hermitage nestled against a curtain of dark green pine trees, and Father Louis was sitting on the lighted porch praying his morning office. Brother Maurice, who looked after the hermitage in Father's absence, Philip Stark, a Jesuit scholastic from Woodstock College who had spent the summer in the Guest House at Gethsemani and who had helped with the typing and layout of *Monks Pond* (a journal of avant-garde poetry edited by Father Louis), and I were invited by Father to join him in his last Mass in the hermitage chapel before he left on his Asian journey.

As we approached the cabin, "Uncle Louie" (his monastic nickname and one which amused him) closed his office book and greeted us warmly. He asked us if we had any special preference for what Mass he would offer. We decided unanimously that it would be the Votive Mass of Saint Peter Claver, which was a great favorite of his. Coincidentally, it turned out to be Phil's birthday, so it was appropriate to have the Mass in honor of a Jesuit saint.

After filling the cruets with water and wine, Father began to vest for Mass, as we lighted the candles. The chapel, which was a more recent addition to the hermitage, was just large enough to accommodate a congregation of three. On the wall above the cedar altar hung a group of five or six icons of varying sizes (one originally came from Mount Athos), and on the floor in front of the altar was a hand-woven Navajo rug, a gift from the Benedictine monks of Christ in the Desert monastery in New Mexico.

We all joined in the Prayers of the Faithful, Phil read the

Epistle, and Father Louis read the beautiful Gospel narrative
of the Good Samaritan, after which he surprised us with a
brief but deeply moving homily. He compared himself to
"the traveler" who had been attacked by robbers and was
then left half dead along the road, and described how we
each in our own way had been Good Samaritans to him,
helping him "to get out of the ditch." He embarrassed us by
expressing his appreciation for all we had done for him (precious little it was!) and he said he was offering the Holy
Sacrifice of the Mass for our intentions.

Before Communion he embraced each of us in the Kiss of
Peace. We received under both Species, and I remember that
he addressed us personally, using our first names: "The Body
of the Lord, Phil, etc." As beautiful and as meaningful a
Mass as I have ever experienced.

After a short thanksgiving we heard "Uncle Louie" in the
kitchen preparing coffee for our breakfast, so we came in
from the porch and got in his way in an effort to help. Places
were set on the wooden table in front of the fireplace, before
the large window overlooking the quiet valley. By now the
sun was beginning to rise behind the knobs in the east, and
there in the joy of the morning, we broke bread with our hermit for the last time.

During our breakfast we gave Father free advice about his
forthcoming trip, over which he was as enthusiastic as a child
in expectation of some wonderful new adventure. Phil and I,
who had spent several years in Rome, cautioned him about
exotic Oriental foods, and how careful he must be. We also
warned him about drinking local tap water, and advised him
to be content with wine or beer with his meals. To this suggestion he agreed wholeheartedly.

He spoke of the various places and people he hoped to visit
on his Asian journey—especially the Dalai Lama and the
Tibetan Buddhist monks now exiled in northern India, for
whom he had the greatest respect and a lively interest. He
was going with an open attitude of listening to them and
learning what he could from this ancient monastic tradition
of the East, as he wrote later: "I hope I can bring back to my

monastery something of the Asian wisdom with which I am
fortunate to be in contact . . ." (see *The Asian Journal of
Thomas Merton*, pp. 320 ff for complete text of this letter).

We cleared off the table and went out on the porch, where
the sun was not very bright. Father Louis remembered that
he had some unused film in his camera, and he began at once
taking pictures of the three of us. We took turns with the
camera so that we had photographs taken with him in front
of the hermitage and in the surrounding woods. When the
last frame of the roll of film was shot we returned to the hermitage and began clearing things up in preparation for his departure. Father gave each of us books and photographs, saying: "Here, Phil, a book for you," one of Victor Hammer's
excellent handprinted books (*Hagia Sophia*), and to me a
copy of *The John Howard Griffin Reader*, which I was
eager to read. A "hermit button" was pinned on Brother
Maurice.

After some last-minute instructions about taking care of his
correspondence during his absence, he handed me his set of
keys to the hermitage and to his post office box, where an
enormous stack of mail was delivered daily. We said goodbye,
never realizing that this would be our last Mass with Father
Louis. With loaded arms, we headed down to the monastery.

This was my last sight of the man of God, who was to me
a Father, a Brother, and a faithful Friend. May the Lord be
rich in rewarding him, "good measure, pressed down, shaken
together and running over. . . ."

P. H.

MATTHEW KELTY

THE MAN

You could tell Father Louis by his walk. He had a rather rapid walk, but not altogether measured and orderly. For one thing, his feet were spread out fan-fashion, and there was something sad in his gait. But it was a vigorous walk, except when he was reading, as he often was. He had small hands and feet (he was very hard on shoes!) and a fine torso with strong shoulders and back. His legs seemed a bit short and this made him look smaller than he really was. Clothes did not suit him well: I mean he never looked neat and spruce, though in his monk's habit he was presentable enough. Things rather hung on him and somehow looked baggy and shapeless. Even when dressed in civilian clothes, he did not look sharp, but a trifle disordered and disorganized. He did not care much about clothes, that was obvious. In the years he was living in his hermitage he would appear at the monastery for dinner and a few appointments in some odd combination of work clothes, generally with an attaché case of mail or books, or a bag of groceries to take back up the hill.

If you stopped to talk to him for a moment, and he was glad enough when you did, he was always wide-awake and intent, looking closely at you with bright and eager eyes, for if he had a plain and even common face, his eyes were rich in life, never far from merriment. His voice was quiet and his laugh gentle, but deep and like a chuckle. He had a way of sensing when something was done and would end the matter there. This was a real characteristic. He loathed dragging things out beyond their measure. When something was finished, he was ready for the next engagement. I recall that in periods of spiritual direction when I was a novice he always seemed to know before I did when the matter was over. It never seemed to me to end without a kind of abruptness, which I had later to admit was simply a quick and sure grasp of the situation: that we had reached a point of terminus. In meetings of the Abbot's private council or the building committee or such groups, he was often ill at ease since they were sometimes long in coming to an end. Windy and drawn-out discussions bored and exasperated him. Even in a casual conversation, if there was no more to be said, he was off. Visitors and callers who had nothing more than chatter or small talk got short shrift with him, but he was always courteous and kind to any with real need. It was not that he was hasty or restless, but he knew "how to get off the phone" and he hated to waste time. He had a great reverence for time, had a sacramental view of it.

He was always totally immersed in what he was doing and never played idly at something which was serious. Thus, in his work, he was systematic and followed regular procedures. He had his work "well organized," as we say. Again, I recall that when I was a novice he would finish assigning us our work after morning chapter and would then go upstairs to his office. Once in a while some question would come up while we were changing clothes to go to work, and one of us would run up to see him: he was generally very short and even curt. He did not like to be bothered once he was into his work and did not mind indicating that such courtesy toward others—leaving them in peace and undisturbed—was the normal thing for a monk. I often worked for him, typing manuscripts or answering mail. Sometimes it was difficult, for his writing was poor, the text hard to make out. You did not like to bother him, and you knew if you did that he would not like it either! In his manuscripts he was very consistent in pattern: he would type the first draft, then go over by hand in blue pen, making corrections and additions. Then later he would go over a second time in black pen, doing the same. Then he would have somebody type it, novices when he was Novice Master. It then got another reading and possibly a few altera-

tions, not many. In all there was method, and once you got
to know his hand and his style for insertions and changes, it
was not too difficult. His biggest problem seemed to be in
keeping things limited, for the more he worked on a script
the bigger it got. He kept getting new insights, new openings.

In the beginning he seemed to write directly for publication, but with the passing years he used to do more and more
for private circulation or for magazines. Following these mimeographed copies and the published articles he would receive
valued comments which helped him a great deal in clarifying
his thinking. Later he would gather related topics into books
and publish them. This formula was almost a general practice
with him in his last years. Even so there was a vast amount of
material that had never been published when he died, much
of it in private manuscript form and in mimeo notes. It is
perhaps characteristic of him that in the writing area everything was in good order when he died, all arranged and taken
care of with great foresight. This fact, with others, led some
to believe that he had some certainty that his end was at
hand. Everything seemed just a little too tidy. In any case,
though in some areas he lacked organization, work was not
one of them.

System was easy to see in him. He liked to have set plans
for what he did at all times of the day: what type of reading,
where he would do it, and so on. He was a typical monk in
liking to save steps and time, would combine things: on his
way to choir mail some letters, check the bulletin board, pick
up a pair of shoestrings, get some razor blades. But he did
this easily and without tension. He was good at keeping appointments. He had an air of dispatch in all he did and generally was thorough, but at times a bit hasty and wanting in
depth. He had very fine insights into people and was a good
judge of men. He sometimes blundered in interviews with
postulants to the monastery, but his overall perception was
far above average. And he could be open in discussion: I
mean able to see another's point of view. Once he had his
mind made up, however, he was hard to change. And being
basically a tender-hearted and gentle person, he sometimes

found duties difficult and would avoid them if he honorably could, but he was no coward and could be straightforward and uncompromising with withering directness. With the novices also he was not at all unwilling to see what they were made of: more than once I myself found that he had a way of testing the spirit, though I entered as a mature priest. Nor was he shy about needed comment: I recall a remark he made to me that last year or so, when we were getting ready for conventual Mass, the Sunday concelebration at which he generally assisted. I must have had a particularly gloomy face and he said to me, "Cheer up, Matt!" Nor was he just trying to give me a pleasant greeting: what he was saying was that I had no business appearing in public with such a long face.

When you consider the vast amount of writing the man did in his lifetime, the total output staggers you. Yet this output was but part of his work, for along with it went a vast amount of reading, both that which was spiritual, strictly speaking, and that which was in connection with his writing. And, up until his years in the hermitage, this was combined with the regular monastic choir. In addition he was Novice Master for the last ten years in the house, and in connection with this did a lot of writing of notes and conferences on the Rule, the monastic Fathers, the history of the Order, monastic spirituality—most of it mimeographed. When you recall that his health was hardly the best and that he never had the services of a regular secretary until just prior to his death, it turns out that he was a veritable work horse. Which is to say that he made very good use of his time.

Even in the old days when the routine called for a noon-time rest, he hated to sleep during the day and generally could not anyway. One of the most popular of his poems, "On the Death of my Brother," was written as he lay on his bed during the siesta time on the day he received the telegram. When he got up he had only to write it down. Yet, it was a matter of control to him. Work time was work time and when it was done, it was done. He was merciless toward novices he found stretching their work beyond the prescribed hours, particularly if there was no need. Nor did he approve of great projects that ate up interval reading time; for instance, he had a horror of extravagant decorations for Christmas or Corpus Christi. He loved the hours of the night for prayer and after he became a hermit spent such night hours in private prayer, doing his office and Mass in daylight. He took a dim view of monks who could not get to bed on time, or for that matter rise on time. He himself was most regular in this. It is true, late retirers often woke him as they climbed the stairs, but it was also a matter of principle to him. For years he had a little room (he slept very poorly) perched over a stairwell off the novitiate dormitory. It was handy, but not too quiet. The farm Brothers also will not soon forget the intensity of his feeling about night-farming: harvesting corn and chopping alfalfa by the light of the moon. The roar of the machinery kept him awake for hours and he was not reluctant to let it be known.

Yet he did not go around the place giving the appearance of great activity. In fact, it is only by sitting down and adding up what he did that you come to the conclusion that the man was a phenomenal worker. There is scarcely anyone in the monastery who comes near him. He was outstanding in work, as also in reading. About books he was fussy, though he read much and widely. He kept in close touch with the library, knew what new books came in, checked the periodicals regularly. When doing some special study he would get books from other libraries and dig into the matter with enthusiasm. For years he made almost daily use of the large volumes of Migne, carting them back to the scriptorium after each session. He was, of course, a good source for books too, since publishers sent him many and he did a lot of reviews. He would send batches of them over every now and then.

He was very interested in community life. In no sense was he a gossip or a busybody, but he knew what was going on and kept his eyes open, missed little. He thought that was a part of life in community, family life. He was never indifferent to his brothers. Even as a hermit he did not dissociate himself from the community, but stayed very much with it in terms of knowledge and interest.

People he loved. But he loved nature too. The latter seemed to play a large role in his life at Gethsemani, and though his love never bore the fruit he perhaps hoped for, it did have great effect and may have far greater effect in days to come. He was passionately fond of the woods and early in his monastic life found means to spend a great deal of time there. In nature he easily found God and he returned thanks in knowledge and care. He knew the woods well: could identify all kinds of wildlife with accuracy. The novices and scholastics under him (he was Master of Scholastics for several years) planted thousands of trees in desolate or washed-out areas. It was through his instigation that the forest service erected a fire tower on one of the hills near the monastery, and he once dreamed of being a kind of forest-ranger-hermit. Yet it must be admitted that with the passing years the monastery's official interest in the woods became less and less apparent. In days gone by we used to get all our firewood from the woods to heat the house and do the cooking and supply steam, but those days have long passed. Once the last wood-burning furnace was gone, the woods more or less ceased to function as a monastery area of concern. The two remaining fireplaces—one in the guest house and one in the monastery—take little wood for their intermittent fires, in comparison with the tremendous appetites of the old furnaces and boilers. The big woodshed at the rear of the house has become a refuge for junk and a place to store farm equipment over the winter. Meanwhile, since the woods were not easily available to the monks, that whole side of the monastery property was left to its own devices, and with that died Fr. Louis's dreams of applied forestry. In the last few years some change has set in: the woods are now open to the monks, there is more interest, and younger people in particular seem more aware of the good the woods have to offer.

Father Louis was partial to the land. He liked farming, though not the kind that Trappist monks are prone to. What might be called "rustic farming" appealed to him: farming, that is, more romantic than practical. He had little love for machinery, and the sound of a tractor in the bottoms roused no poetry in him. He could become very grim about poisons and sprays and what these things did, do, or might do, to wildlife. Nor was he unwilling to pass these observations on. Basically, his view of the world of agriculture was more that of a poet than that of a farmer, and the response of the farmers was the obvious one: you cannot make much of a living from poetry. Still, all are aware, farmers too, that many sins against God and the world God made give point to his misgivings. Violence against nature was to his soul as much a distortion as violence against man: the distant boom of the guns in Fort Knox was no more comfort to him than a military jet shattering the sound barrier overhead or a droning bulldozer changing the course of Monks' Creek. All his days he kept a love for all things living. Shy deer used to graze in the meadow beyond the fence of rambler roses at his door, and when I used to work with the thoroughbred horses we boarded, he asked me if some of them could not be pastured in the field next to his hermitage. I recall that one summer I had a chance to do some mowing and ended up doing his fields as he requested. It happened that in the process I inadvertently chopped a few little fir trees he had planted. He was very indignant. . . . I do not mean to imply that he went through life with a kind of eagle-eye on the lookout for violations against his world, but rather that the heart of him was easily roused when a heavy hand was laid on any of the good earth.

He was not anti-machine. He had a respect for machines and what they could do for mankind. He admired a good typewriter and was quite aware of the shoddy work in some of the late models. He admired the Brothers who were capable of making wonderful things, and had numerous friends who were craftsmen and artisans. But just as he grieved over man's use of his magnificent achievements for nothing better than war, so he also took offense at violence done the natural world. All in all, though, it must probably be admitted that his interest in the woods and the fields never really caught on in the monastery, though a coming generation may respond to that vision. At present there are some signs of this.

We must admit also that, being agrarian in spirit, he was not charmed by monastic industries, those means by which monks support themselves. He was indeed almost unkind in his comments on our local cheese and fruit cake complex, and could get eloquent on this invasion of monastic life by the assembly line and production management. The complex remains, of course, and will, but that it is modest and well in hand may without doubt be laid to his influence. Had he been abbot, I daresay the problem of income might have been a serious one! But he no doubt would have given that whole area over to those competent in it, which is to say that things would probably be just about as they are. Incidentally, in this matter of being abbot, in our election not long before his death he was aware that there were some in the community who were looking in his direction. The idea filled him with genuine confusion, not the mock-humility of those who assure you of their unworthiness with tones that sound a little forced, but in the truest sense of the word. For he knew himself, knew that he was variable, apt to take off on tangents, somewhat temperamental and effervescent. He knew he was not too good at organization and in practical affairs, though in this he exaggerated his lacks. So he wrote a note to the community, trying to be light-hearted and merry about it, though he was quite in earnest. As it turned out, some of the brethren thought he was being sarcastic in refusing to serve as abbot over such a weird crew! This reaction only confirmed him in his self-study.

His place in the community was as a monk among monks. No one made anything of him. He neither expected special handling nor got it. This does not mean that he adopted some sort of humble manner by which he managed to hide his own importance. On the contrary, he was very much himself, very alive and very real. When you met him, spoke with him, had dealings with him, you never felt you were dealing with something artificial: quite the opposite. He was nothing if not real. And part of that reality was his simplicity, his being himself. He said what he thought and did what he thought should be done, and that was all there was to it. And what he said and what he did was rooted in love for God and man. No one here ever thought of him as famous, a great author, a renowned personality. The basic reason for that was that he did not think of himself that way. He did not make a big thing of his writings, and once they came out he never read them again. He did not go out of his way to be humble about them, to speak disparagingly about them: he simply did not see them in that light. He knew he was a writer, he knew he was a successful writer, he knew he was a name. But to him, making something of that would be like a priest priding himself for his priesthood. Indeed, as with his priesthood, he saw his whole life as a calling from God and one he was bound to answer faithfully. The calling did not make him: it was how he answered it that mattered. He tried to answer it with all he had.

He had no special ways of manners, did not cultivate a personality. Actually, he enjoyed doing the opposite; that is, he did as the others did. Though he had a miserable digestive system, suffered much from it, he was no crank, nor did he have a reputation with the Brothers in the kitchen for the infirm for being fussy or demanding. The community responded to this total simplicity just as you would expect: they treated him as they would any of the monks. They loved him, accepted him, absorbed him. But they never made a cult of him. Never.

Not that he was spineless and without ability to take a stand, even an unpopular one! He took his place in the community, which is to say that he made his own contributions, his own comments on the local scene. He let it be known when he thought something was stupid. He did not mind saying so if a ceremony was too long and involved, a sermon endless, a project foolish. In the matter of his hermit vocation he was particularly persistent and courageous. Looking back over the years and years of patient effort in the direction of this call one can only marvel. In working it out, he literally had mountains of opposition to overcome. He simply wore those mountains down by prayer, by suffering, by patience. It is something of a wonder today to see a monk take up the hermit vocation, here in the Abbey for example, with no more trouble than is involved in asking for it, when we recall that this man obtained as much only by dint of staggering efforts over a long period of time.

Thus: first he had a few hours in the woods, but even that only after long discussion and arrangements; a "job" was created for him so that he could be in the woods: "forestry." Even when he got his little hermitage on the hill, time in it was doled out in little bits and pieces: a few hours in the morning or in the afternoon, but never over dinner. Or later, all day long once in a while, but never overnight. Or when he could stay overnight, never with Holy Mass up there. Or when he finally got to say Mass there, never with the Holy Sacrament reserved. And so on. He was a very patient man. But let it be remembered, to keep the thing in proper context, that the Abbot with whom he was working out this vocation was also the one who rose in the General Chapter to speak movingly in behalf of the eremetical calling within the Order. And effectively.

The monks, of course, were never really keen on the hermit idea. Some were. Some were even enthusiastic. Some, however, took great exception to it and never approved of it. The majority simply accepted it as "one of those things" and were not excited one way or the other. But a kind of abiding minority opinion always remained opposed. Thus, even a few weeks before he left for the Far East, there was a mild flare-up of talk against hermits. He took issue with it and discussed it with some of those concerned. Nor did he hesitate to inform one official that if they did not want him around here there were other places he could go and receive welcome. And he meant this. And, admittedly, it was true: many had offered him place and would have been very happy to have him. He was, after all, no fool, and he did not like being treated unfairly. That some of these champions of the cenobitic life were themselves scarcely models did not escape his droll notice either. It was not that this embittered him, but it did hurt him. In terms of his service to the community it was truly rather shabby treatment, but that was not his

point. He was not asking for the hermit life as a reward for
services rendered. To him it was simply part of the monastic
life, monastic life also in the Cistercian tradition. And in this
he knew what he was talking about.

He always encouraged those who felt themselves called to
solitude but on the other hand was aware that it was not for
everyone. In his mind, the actual hermit calling would always be something only a few would be interested in. Others
might feel some attraction and would find that times of solitude were all that they needed. For the far greater number,
he was quite aware that life within the enclosure would be
the thing, but even within this framework he stressed freedom and elbow-room.

He was not the most practical of men. For the Brothers
this was always a cause of mild and good-natured amusement.
He could not drive a car, and some few efforts in this direction were disconcerting. He was not handy with tools.
Though he loved the woods and growing things, he was almost dangerous with an axe, and even puttering around the
house with lawns and flowers was not something he was very
good at. He was no cook, and his kitchen left perhaps something to be desired in terms of neatness and cleanliness. It
was for this reason that Dom James insisted that he come
down to the monastery (fifteen minutes' walk) for his dinner: that way he would get at least one good meal a day. He
could make a good pot of tea, but I would not have trusted
his cooking much beyond that.

His little hermitage was fairly comfortable in the end. It
had a long room across the front of the house, with lots of
large windows and a view of the bottom lands and the hills
south. There was a large fireplace. To the rear, two rooms:
one a kitchen and work room, one a bedroom. Later a chapel
was added, and a bathroom. It was adequate but hardly more
than that, being simple concrete block. It could be drafty and
no doubt when he had only the fireplace and used an outdoor
privy, he suffered a little. But he had propane heat later and
electricity and this made the place most habitable. Even so,
when he last saw it, there were still a few small jobs to be

taken care of, so in a sense he never saw it finished. A well had been dug a year or two before, but the water was not good for drinking, so water was brought to him, though for a time he used to take a gallon jug along when he went home. I mention all these trifles to show you that we did not fuss over him. He was treated just as the other monks and this was so because that is the way he wanted it. He did not ask for this, did not describe to us how we should treat him. We simply reacted to what he was. He thought of himself in modest terms and it never occurred to us to think of him in any other.

Thus, he was asked by the abbot to give open talks in chapter on Sunday afternoons. This was after he had gone to live in his hermitage; previous to that, when he was Novice Master, his Sunday conferences were always open to any of the monks who wished to attend. So the custom began. The attendance was good, perhaps thirty or forty or more—about a third of the monks. The talks were excellent, covered a wide range from the mystical life to contemporary literature and usually ran in a series. But the monks did not flock to them, nor did he expect them to. Had they stopped coming in any number he would simply have quit giving the talks without ado and that would have been all right with him. The very fact that the monks sensed this "take it or leave it" attitude speaks much for the man. He never wanted a "following," and even as Novice Master was ruthless in avoiding this. He wanted to lead men to God, to a good monastic life, but never to Thomas Merton. In this he could be very fierce. He had a multitude of friends and they meant much to him, but he would have no one clinging to him.

One must say something of his obedience. He did not find obedience easy. He had a passionate love for freedom, yet he understood the role of authority and submission to it in the plan of salvation. He certainly understood its role in the monastery. Though he was not at all unwilling to criticize what he thought an unwarranted use of this authority, he knew what authority was, what it was for, and what a monk's response to it should be. He was very obedient. Once he knew what the superior wanted, that was it. Up to that point he was capable of argument, but once the stand was taken, he accepted it. And for him this was scarcely a once-in-a-while experience. He was the son of artists, was himself a poet, had all the romantic tendencies of the artistic temperament. His dreams, plans, ideas were manifold. He would submit them one after another as they came up, and watch the original interested response gradually cool and settle at last into the usual negative reply. It was almost a ritual with him. Under it he sometimes chafed and no doubt suffered much, but he knew what he was about. He had feelings that perhaps this after all was the best thing for him and these feelings in later years grew into solid convictions. If on the one side we say that the Abbot held the reins tight, there is small doubt that there was any other way to do it with such a man. Even Father Louis, in the end, was grateful for the guidance given him and realized that submission to the rule and to the Abbot had been his salvation. His last trip—the one to Bangkok—was really his first. Yet it had not been the first to suggest itself. It was only the last of many such. It turned out, appropriately, that this first should also be his last. But how many others there were! How many schemes and dreams!*

There were those who smiled forgivingly at all these boyish vagaries, of course, but they may have missed the man's great courage and follow-through. An idea, an inspiration, to him was not an idle matter, something to toy with. He saw response and action as necessarily called for. It was this brave spirit that was his outstanding quality. He took a stand. He had a point of view. He took sides. And he followed perfectly the monastic ideal in submitting all things to his Abbot. It took phenomenal fortitude (and a phenomenal Abbot?). Nor

---

* Thomas Merton made three trips outside the monastery during the period when Abbot James Fox was superior: in the mid-fifties there was a journey to Columbus, Ohio, in search of a new foundation for Gethsemani; in 1956 he attended a psychological workshop at St. John's Abbey, Collegeville, Minnesota, along with his abbot and Father John Eudes Bamberger; and in 1964, he traveled to New York for a meeting with the late Dr. Daisetz Suzuki.—EDITOR.

was he blind to the timidity so many manifested. Monks who have little love for silence, for fasting, for work, for intimate prayer, for inner poverty, for solitude, depressed and disappointed him, as cowards playing with the monastic life. Nor was he unaware that some used his own free spirit as a convenient model for the casual approach. Most of his monastic life he neither fasted nor abstained, on account of his poor health. He could be friendly and engaging in conversation with anyone. Nor was he above drinking a can of beer sometimes. He had many visitors and was often at the gate, or in town, especially in later years. He led his own life and had little truck with an effort to edify people. People truly found in him what they were looking for. He was totally committed to the monastic life, but he insisted that if its ascesis did not spring from within the man, it was of little use, and of no use if only imposed. Obviously he was much misunderstood here and he realized it, but there was no other way.

It was this free spirit that gave rise to the rumors that he had left the monastery. These plagued him all his life. There were always comments arising somewhere in the press that he had been seen at such and such a place: that he was teaching in Paris or living in New York, that he had left the Church. These always saddened him. He had a profound love for Holy Church, for the priesthood, for the monastic life, for Gethsemani. He had indeed over the years thought of many things: the various other Benedictine observances, the Camaldolese, the Carthusians; thought of a remote hermitage somewhere in distant mountains, had a hankering for South America that really never left him. Even when he left for his journey to the Far East, with his tongue in his cheek he said, "I just might find me a lonely spot and settle down there." Yet in all these visions, there was at bottom a primary search for God's holy will and a willingness to respond to it without qualification of any kind. But because he spoke and wrote easily of these longings and liked to hear them out loud that he might better understand them, he was often misinterpreted by realistic and pragmatic people who thought him basically thwarted and unhappy. He had instead the docility of

a child and the simple kind of happiness a child has. Yet the
knowledge that so many had little confidence in him did dis-
appoint him. He accepted this humbly, knowing very well
that as he set out for the East the papers would say that he
had left the Order, etc. They did.

So, if the Abbot was somewhat hard on him, he knew
what he was about. No one who is unwilling to die with the
Lord in this religious experience is a disciple of Father Louis.
He was an obedient monk and in this relationship to the
Abbot he saw the elemental structure of the monastic life. If
we do not read this lesson in his life, we have not read him
well. But let no superior rest comfortably in his seat with the
blessings of Father Louis on him, for the man could burn
with a prophet's fire against those who misused authority and
threw their weight around with reckless abandon. He was
quite aware of what they have done to the Church and to religion.

His work in the field of writing gives evidence of the same
spirit, for he suffered much from censors over the years. It
would seem that in the beginning they were especially
difficult but as time went on became more benign. But even
in his last years it was not always easy going nor were the
paths pleasant. It grieved him that his book on peace had
been turned down even before being censored; but not long
afterwards *Pacem in Terris* appeared, so he was consoled.
When he thought he was being treated unfairly, he said so,
but did as bidden. When someone once commented on the
beauty of a chapter in *Disputed Questions* as one of the best
things he had ever written, his wry answer was, "It should be
good. That chapter was written and rewritten I don't know
how many times to please the censors." I would imagine,
though, that he was sometimes rather warm in his contact
with authority. Lacking direct contact they may have thought
of him as more formidable than he was.

It was perhaps at his death, and the funeral and burial following, that the true dimensions of Gethsemani's relations
with Father Louis became manifest. It is rare for a monastic
funeral to have such an impact as his had. It is not that in

the death of other monks we were less concerned with love, for there is genuine love here, but the intensity of this particular experience escaped no one. And it was as was the man himself, a combination of contradictions. For it was very sad and grief-ridden, but at the same time something brim-filled with joy and a kind of rapture. I have never in my life assisted at such a joyous funeral: it was more of a wedding celebration! And yet the anguish of knowing that he was no longer with us was a great weight on the heart. All in all, it was a community experience of great love, a testimony to the great mystery of love among us in the power of Christ, a love hidden in some way, yet there, as the great inner reality, the core of our life together. The comings and goings, the agreements and the differences, the gives and the takes, the brightness and the dullness, the stupid and the silly as well as the brilliant and the accomplished—the whole fabric of the life of day to day was laid bare, and there for all to see was this glorious presence of love behind it all, beneath it all. It was evident that the man loved us. And it was evident that we loved him. And this love is the evidence of the presence of Christ.

There is in these remarks the note of the disparity of reaction to Father Louis. I think this is important. It describes his life among us in somewhat the same dimensions as his life in the Church, in the world. He was a kind of dividing spirit, a sign spoken against, a sort of question demanding an answer. Thus, he raised issues, and there was no way out but to reply one way or other. In this he was unsettling, disturbing, not comfortable to live with. Put in other words, there was a kind of truth about him that got under your skin, into your heart. He belonged to nobody, free as a bird. He could not be categorized, labeled, pigeonholed. And he had vision. Putting this together makes it clear that the fire in him burned not only himself, but burned many around him as well. A sort of prophetic fire, the fire Christ came to cast on the earth, and called on this man to cast. We monks of Gethsemani must be forgiven if we could not always abide this fire of the Lord among us. We did the best we could. We tried very hard. And I think, by and large, that we succeeded. He was a great gift of God, and yet we had some share in that gift, we had our part to play. I think we stood the test well. Father Louis was true to Gethsemani to the end. And I say with confidence also: and Gethsemani was true to Father Louis. The rest is in the hands of God and lies written in his books.

JOHN EUDES BAMBERGER

THE MONK

In Bangkok, just a few hours before his death, Thomas Merton made what proved to be his final autobiographical comment. It is altogether characteristic that his remarks took the form of a statement of identity. "I am a monk. I shall remain a monk until death. Nothing can stop me from being one."

This statement was not delivered without deep feeling. It was neither casual nor an isolated one of its kind. Ever since leaving on his Asian journey he was concerned to make his position clear with respect to his monastic vocation. "Give my regards to all the gang," he wrote to Gethsemani a few weeks after his departure in September, "and I hope there are not too many crazy rumors. Keep telling everyone that I am a monk of Gethsemani and intend to remain one all my days."*

He was somewhat sensitive on this point and not without reason. Over the years he had been alternately vexed and amused at the persistent rumors that had him outside the monastery, the Order, and even the priesthood. He knew that once he actually did travel for an extended period there would be a plethora of such tales and a consequent misrepresentation of his whole aim and purpose in traveling to the East.

Predictably, some journalistic accounts have spoken of him as having "wandered back into the world" just as he had "wandered into the monastery" in the first place. In reality,

---

* This letter, dated September 26, 1968, from Anchorage, Alaska, was one of the first of a series of twenty-eight letters which Father Merton wrote to his secretary, Brother Patrick Hart, at Gethsemani in the course of his trip.—EDITOR

Merton was one of the most "stabilized" monks in history. Until the last few years, when he visited physicians in town fairly often, he was almost constantly on the monastic grounds. When he did make a trip in 1956 it was in order to go to St. John's monastery, and he went in the company of his abbot and a monk (myself). His travels the last year of his life involved a couple of visits to monasteries. Hardly an exciting travelogue.

Yet he continued all along to be pursued by stories of his lost vocation, or of having separated himself from his community at Gethsemani. He decided to comment on the situation, finally in 1963, when he wrote the preface to the Japanese edition of *The Seven Storey Mountain:* "Many rumors have been disseminated about me since I came to the monastery. Most of them have assured people that I had left the monastery, that I had returned to New York, that I was in Europe, that I was in South America or Asia, that I had become a hermit, that I was married, that I was drunk, that I was dead" (p. 9).

I myself had run across many of these rumors. When traveling in Europe as a student it was not rare to be told "Merton has left Gethsemani, I hear. He has gone to the Galapagos" (or some such place).

In this same passage Fr. Louis went on to make a formal denial of the instability of his monastic vocation, in the most explicit terms: "Certainly I have never for a moment thought of changing the definitive decisions taken in the course of my life: to be a Christian, to be a monk, to be a priest. If anything, the decision to renounce and to depart from modern secular society, a decision repeated and reaffirmed many times, has finally become irrevocable" (*ibid.*, p. 9).

A little later, in a different context of the same article he averred still more forcibly: "I am still in the monastery, and intend to stay there. I have never had any doubt whatsoever of my monastic vocation. If I have ever had a desire for change, it has been for a more solitary, and more 'monastic' way" (*ibid.*, p. 11). It was, apparently, incredible to many

people that Merton could ever find in monastic life enough
to keep him in the monastery for long. Certainly, anyone
who was acquainted with men and affairs could hardly be
reproached for exhibiting a degree of scepticism about his
remaining in one place indefinitely. No one could have
predicted that he would remain in the same monastic community, composed of quite ordinary men, for twenty-seven
years, to the very end of his life.

For one thing Merton had an impulsive, enthusiastic temperament—*überschwenglich*, exuberant, was the apt term Jean
Leclercq used to describe him. He was anything but a "team
man" and submission to a superior was considerably less con-
natural to him than, say, flying, planeless, in the air. There
always remained a certain ill-defined, latent air of daring
about him that conveyed the distinct impression of unpredic-
tability. A quality that led one to feel, "What might he do
next?" His temperament, at once energetic and gregarious,
and his broad and varied culture made the most diverse kind
of international society congenial to him. It turned out that,
even though Bardstown is somewhat removed from the
American mainline for foreign visitors, there was a steady
stream of persons of multifarious interests coming to speak
with him from all over the world. He counted among his
friends Vietnamese Buddhists, Hindu monks, Japanese Zen-
masters, Sufi mystics, professors of religion and mysticism
from Jerusalem's University, French philosophers, artists and
poets from Europe, South America, and the States, Arabic
scholars, Mexican sociologists, and many others. He was not
only at home with all these men, he was on most friendly
terms with each, and anyone who has been at the informal
meetings he held with them over the years recognized how
much pleasure he took in such company.

In spite of his deep unvarying and intense attraction to solitude Father Louis was one of the most sociable of men, who
had an absolute need for human society. Not a compulsive
need, by any means. I do not in the least suggest that he
could not dominate this need, still less that it was leading

him around by the nose. Only that when he was most himself, and in order to be most himself, he would require, with considerable regularity, to meet with people with whom he could converse on subjects of the most diversified kind and with whom he could be simply present. As intense as his longing for solitude and silence was—and this too was a very real, urgent necessity for him—it had always struck me that in an out-and-out battle, if it ever came to that, his social instinct would easily win the day. As victor in such a battle, however, he would have never reconciled himself to the ensuing pace, for life without solitude would have been unendurable. And I suppose that is why, in fact, a pitched battle never developed. The entrenched, semiconscious conflict between these two needs remained, active and intense, till the end.

It does not take a highly endowed imagination to fancy what the consequences of this kind of complexity were for Merton himself, first of all, in terms of community life. And also, at times, for his brethren, and especially, his abbot.

If Father Louis was to live and die as a monk who remained a member of Gethsemani for his entire monastic career it would not be as a consequence of his natural gifts and tendencies.

The monastic life has never been seen, by monks at least, as suited only to certain temperaments and not to others, in any exclusive way. A monastic vocation is essentially a matter of grace. It transcends psychological, social, and cultural levels of life in its ultimate requirements, though obviously its concrete realization is closely bound to them. Essentially, then, a vocation is a matter of a personal call and the vivid account Merton gave of the circumstances of his own call to the monastic life leaves no room to doubt but that he experienced his own vocation precisely as a call. Indeed, it was literally the calling of the bells of Gethsemani that gave him the conviction, at a critical moment, of his vocation as a monk.

Suddenly, as soon as I had made that prayer, I became aware of the wood, the trees, the dark hills, the wet night wind, and then, clearer than any of these obvious realities, in my imagination, I started to hear the great bell of Geth-semani ringing in the night—the bell in the big grey tower, ringing and ringing, as if it were just behind the first hill. . . .

The bell seemed to be telling me where I belonged—as if it were *calling me home*. (*The Seven Storey Mountain*, pp. 364–65, emphasis added)

In later years these same bells seemed to him to be the voice of Christ, at once the bridegroom of the Canticle and the awesome judge of the apocalypse.

> When the full fields begin to smell of sunrise
> And the valleys sing in their sleep,
> . . . from the frowning tower, the windy belfry,
> Sudden the bells come, bridegrooms,
> And fill the echoing dark with love and fear.
>   (The Trappist Abbey: Matins)

Even though his monastic vocation was understood and ex-perienced by Merton as beyond cultural norms and forms, yet he was obviously wholly involved in precisely these levels of life, as few other men of our times were. He knew very well how little, on these levels, he conformed to the ready-made image of a monk, least of all of a "holy" monk. "As an icon I'm not doing so good," he wrote (*Conjectures of a Guilty Bystander*) with no indication whatsoever of being repentant for the fact. Iconoclastic propensities not only flowered in his spirit as if in their natural habitat, he cultivated them with boundless satisfaction.

At the same time he also was an image-maker, and though the pattern he followed in leading his own monastic life was hard to make out at times, even for himself, he fully realized that it was part of his vocation not only to live the monastic life himself, but in living it to remake for his times the image of what a monk was. And to do this especially with other monks in mind, chiefly the young monks to whom the future belonged.

There was nobody less solemn than he, and refusal to conform to ready-made images included the popular concept of
the Merton-image: "the fact that I have a name. Does this
mean I am expected to produce a certain habitual presence
which corresponds to this name? . . . I protest" ("Day of a
Stranger"). He certainly did not set out, consciously, to create
a new "monk-image." Such a program would have been
completely out of style and out of character. But he was
aware that, as he faithfully lived out his own vocation, he
would be, for many people, destroying old images and creat-
ing new ones, and he realized that this was a part of his vocation, an added dimension of it, as invariable as a man's
shadow in the sun.

He did not blame those who circulated the rumors about
his leaving the monastery or the monastic life, though at
times it was painful that men did not display more
confidence in him. He knew better than others how unlikely
a monk he was. That knowledge was an element that determined the specific way and the intensity with which he experienced his vocation in fact, that is to say as a gratuitous gift
of God, as sheer mercy, and his continuing perseverance as a
continual, personal turning of God to him in gracious love.
"I feel that my own life is especially sealed with this great
sign [of Jonas], which baptism and monastic profession
and priestly ordination have burned into the roots of my
being, because like Jonas himself I find myself traveling toward my destiny in the belly of a paradox" (*The Sign of
Jonas*, The Motto). Solitude itself is a gift of God's compassion: "Your compassion singles out and separates the one on
whom Your mercy falls, and sets him apart from the multi-
tudes. . . ." Paradoxical it might be, but his vocation was
the form in which he knew the mercy of God, and it became
more than a profession, it was his life, his very identity,
though it remained as complex as was his own character. "I
have always overshadowed Jonas with My mercy. . . . Have
you had sight of Me, Jonas My child? Mercy within mercy,
within mercy" (*The Sign of Jonas*, p. 362).

WHERE THE FIELDS END AND THE STARS BEGIN:
THE GEOGRAPHY OF FREEDOM

> Would you seek to trace me?
> Ha! Try catching the tempest
> In a net
>   (Kukoku. Haiku Death-poem)

In his autobiography Father Louis has described something
of what Gethsemani meant to him. He entitled this section
of *The Seven Storey Mountain*, "The Sweet Savor of Liberty." The monastery meant liberation to him in his early
years as a monk. In spite of the vicissitudes of the years and
inevitable modification of his early impressions, it always retained that meaning: "The monastery is a school—a school in
which we learn from God how to be happy. Our happiness
consists in sharing the happiness of God, the perfection of
His unlimited freedom, the perfection of His love" (p. 372).
He spoke more intimately in his journal concerning the community of Gethsemani and the place it played in his life.

> But afterwards [i.e. after solemn profession] I was left
> with a profoundly clean conviction that I had done the
> right thing . . . beyond that the nearest thing to sensible
> consolation was a deep and warm realization that I was im-
> mersed in my community. I am part of Gethsemani. I be-
> long to the family. It is a family about which I have no il-
> lusions. And the most satisfying thing about this sense of
> incorporation is that I am glad to belong to this commu-
> nity, not another, and to be bred flesh and bone into the
> same body as these brothers and not other ones. (*The Sign
> of Jonas*, p. 32)

It was inevitable that someone with Merton's temperament
would find community life rough sailing at times. He was too
creative and too independent and too energetic to fit into any
group smoothly for long, in spite of his best intentions.

For one thing his whole instinct made him keenly sensitive
to all forms of community life. Anything inauthentic he
found highly repellent. Not only in personal relations but es-

pecially in "the institution." Though he had become remarkably tolerant of human weaknesses of most kinds, yet he did not suffer fools gladly, and certain rather common forms of human foolishness that many of us take for granted grated sharply on him.

In addition he had always exercised himself in social criticism. From the time he was fifteen years old he deliberately cultivated his talent for satire and other forms of social "attack." "From the first moment when I discovered that one was not only allowed to make fun of English middle class notions and ideals but encouraged to do so in that bright little drawing room, where we balanced coffee-cups on our knees, I was very happy" (*The Seven Storey Mountain*, p. 79).

This was a source of happiness he never felt altogether called upon to renounce.

He did not hesitate to make use of his considerable powers for criticism—the force of which had to be experienced to be believed—upon his own community, his beloved fathers and brothers. When in the sixties he emerged as one of the most prominent and effective social critics of the political and racial policies pursued by our country it came as a surprise to some who knew him as a poet and a "monk." But he had been gaining experience in the genre over the years in his monastery. Few of us were similarly surprised. If it was a prophetic calling—and most of us felt it was, even though at times we qualified as targets—it was one he was suited for by nature, training, and preference. We learned that living with a prophet was usually profitable, often interesting, and occasionally exasperating.

He could be unfair at times in some of his criticism, not always managing to maintain an adequate perspective and so overlooking limitations imposed by circumstances or personal limits of individuals.

However, the chief impression that Father Louis made on his fellow monks was that he was a true brother. In our community he was surely one of the best loved of people. His whole manner was open and outgoing and so constantly enthusiastic that he quickly formed community. Many of us as

young monks came to feel that he was a friend and spiritual
father. Behind his criticism, his directness, and his inde-
pendence there was a great deal of obvious integrity and of
human affection. He was moved by an immense élan for all
that pertained to the contemplative and monastic life.
Though he continually stressed solitude, silence, and meditation yet he did so in an atmosphere of human warmth and
wholesome insistence on the demands of good relations
among the brethren. In spite of his steady complaints about
being too busy with writing, direction, and teaching it was evident that he enjoyed all three. His conferences were always
very thoroughly worked out in advance and invariably full of
enthusiastic interest for his topic. He led discussions
brilliantly, and with an easy firmness kept things right on the
subject at hand. He was always much appreciated for these
conferences, which continued for eighteen years, regularly.

He had very few inhibitions about discussing with students
any problems or disorders that arose, and one of the things
that kept the boat rocking in the community of students at
Gethsemani besides his social critique (which came as a
steady diet) was his open discussion of his recurrent temptations to leave Gethsemani and become a hermit someplace or
other. I recall entering his office one day when he was reading
a long letter. "Look at this," he said, showing me the letter.
"It just came from Cardinal Valeri [Prefect of the Congregation of Religious]. He turned me down. Can't go to the
Camaldolese. He quotes my own writings against it. [Cf. No
Man Is an Island, p. 138: 'Our Father in Heaven has called
us each one to the place in which He can best satisfy His
infinite desire to do us good.'] Pretty good, don't you think!
That makes it proxima fidei, doesn't it?"

One incident has always stood out in my own memory as
characterizing the spirit of Father Louis's attitude to his novices and students better than any other. Shortly after my leaving the novitiate and commencing my studies, Fr. Louis,
being Magister Spiritus, was my spiritual director. I was still
finding monastic life difficult to accept in those days and was
somewhat defensive in my first talks with him; that is, I was

giving him a hard time. He sized up the situation pretty quickly and at the end of the session, as I was leaving, he suddenly rose to his feet and with unmatched enthusiasm and warmth came out with "Isn't it great that we are in this thing together!"

Recently I received a letter from a nun who was quite upset with some things she had heard about Father Louis from a priest who had met him on the Asian trip. Merton, it was alleged, was in a state of crisis in his last months of life, and the priest, who felt he had good evidence for this view, was convinced it was fortunate he had died when he did. Otherwise he would surely have left his Order and perhaps the priesthood. But most serious of all, and chief evidence for this state of crisis, were the highly uncharitable remarks he had been making about his own monastic community. Fr. Louis had been asked about the renewal of monasticism. Had it been accepted at Gethsemani, was there evidence of understanding of aggiornamento there? Fr. Louis: "Oh sure, they're doing great. They now have cornflakes for breakfast."

How, she wrote, could he be the holy mystic she had come to respect so deeply through his books and go around speaking in this vein about his own community?

My own reaction to this letter was mild surprise that anyone would find such a statement remarkable on the lips of our beloved brother in view of the fact that ever since I've known him he has let fly at us with similar satirical barbs face to face. Having tested some of the brethren's reactions it is now clear that I have not simply become insensitive. They all observed with a laugh: "That's our Fr. Louis!" One of them was the Abbot.

At about the same time he was delivering himself of this and occasional other "indelicate nothings" concerning our brotherhood he was writing things like the following to Gethsemani, on December 8 (i.e., two days before his death).

I think of you all on this Feast Day [The Immaculate Conception] and with Christmas approaching I feel homesick for Gethsemani. But I hope to be at least in a

monastery—Rawa Sening. Also I look forward to being at
[our monastery at] Hong Kong and may be seeing our
three volunteers there (or is it two?) [Two monks of
Gethsemani helping out at Lantao]. No more for the moment. Best love to all.

                                                              Louie

One might properly ask at this juncture: "When does
complexity become ambivalence?"

But perhaps it is more to the point to question oneself as
to whether he too might not have stoned the prophets had
he lived closely with one of them.

ELIAS IS HIS OWN WILD BIRD: IDENTITY AS FREEDOM

As Merton himself has told us, the monastery as a particular place and the monastic community as a specific group of
men had a great deal of significance for him. Some of his
finest writing, especially poetry, was inspired by Gethsemani.
The closing of *The Sign of Jonas*, which, in the form of a
prose-poem, is a meditation inspired by the monastic setting
and the life in the monastery, was called by Maritain one of
the finest passages in modern literature. The monastery as a
home and the monks as brothers had all the deeper hold on
him for the fact that in his earlier life he had never really felt
he had a home, as he told one of us not too long ago. He
"grew up in dormitories," as he put it.

However, all this is but one aspect of the picture. There is
another which is more profound and more explicitly essential
to his vocation, as in fact is the case for every monk with a
true monastic vocation. Merton himself has been very explicit
on the point, even forceful: "My monastery is not a home. It
is not a place where I am rooted and established on the
earth. It is not an environment in which I become aware of
myself as an individual, but rather a place in which I disappear from the world as an object of interest in order to be everywhere in it by hiddenness and compassion. To exist everywhere I have to be a No-one" (Preface to the Japanese
edition of *The Seven Storey Mountain*.)

This is an important passage for understanding Merton's

last years. The idea was there from the beginning, of course. The final poetic passage of his autobiography deals with the same theme—the theme of knowledge of God and sympathy with men through "disappearing." But it is articulated in different language, and the difference in words, for Merton, is significant. It reflects an increased sharpness of focus and stronger emphasis. This formulation is based upon an increased concern with the great issue that finally led him to the East, the problem—and the mystery—of the Transcendent Self, the No-one who has gone beyond the individual self by compassion and purity of love and humility and who is, consequently, united with all. This mystery of self-transcendence became the central concern of his last years.

Before going on to discuss this theme further there is one other point about this passage that deserves notice. It stands in flat verbal contradiction to what he had said earlier about his monastery. "I am part of Gethsemani. I belong to the family."

Merton's writings teem with such contradictory statements. It is a regular feature of his style. This dialectical approach in dealing with life, where one assertion is negated by another, is more than a mere question of psychological ambivalence, though doubtless there was some of that in it. In contrast with psychological ambivalence, however, this feature was more in evidence as he grew more confident of himself and appears with increasing frequency in his later writings. He came to surpass Emerson in his conviction that a man need not trouble himself overmuch about charges of inconsistency so long as he pursued, intuitively, his deepest truth in the confidence that the over-all pattern of his life would witness to an ultimate authenticity and truth.

This is not the place to analyze all the components of this striking feature of Merton's whole life-style. That will be one of the more delicate tasks of his biographer. I merely note here the love of paradox and his playfulness that were so prominent in the pattern. So was his exuberance, which forever led him to make the most absolute statements about all kinds of subjects whether in conversations or in interviews. It is fortunate he did not have the chance to have more press conferences than the one he participated in while in California.

A prominent authority on Zen told me that Merton's remarks at this press conference would be found quite offensive to the Japanese—whom Merton loved best, perhaps, of all the people on earth. He was betrayed, by a momentary enthusiasm for something or other, into overstating his reservations about some of the cultural forms of Zen.

I might venture to add here that he was surely abetted in his natural propensity for a daring spontaneity by certain features of Zen and, more deeply perhaps, by some of the Taoist doctrine, both of which lent a kind of divine sanction to his native style. No doubt it was, in part, this character of spontaneity and the down to earth, concrete, and humorous element in Zen as much as its techniques of meditation that gave it such appeal to him. And the absolute confidence in life in all its multifarious diversity as being ultimately its own justification beyond any superimposed pattern devised by human custom or thought shown by the Taoists fit right in with his own turn of spirit and accounted for his attraction to their school.

Merton, in fact, wrote a book on one of the greatest of the Taoist philosophers, Chuang Tzŭ. He describes him as "a thinker who is subtle, funny, provocative, and not easy to get at"—in other words, a mirror image of Merton, who doubtless unconsciously identified with him so that it is hardly astonishing to find him avowing that "I have enjoyed writing this book more than any other I can remember" (*The Way of Chuang Tzŭ*, pp. 9–10). Here is a passage in which he sums up a key point of Chuang's doctrine on the complementarity of opposites: "Life is a continual development. All beings are in a state of flux. Chuang Tzŭ would have agreed with Herakleitos. What is impossible today may suddenly become possible tomorrow. . . . To cling to one partial view, one limited and conditioned opinion, and to treat this as the ultimate answer to all questions is simply to obscure the Tao" (*ibid.*, p. 30).

This exuberant spontaneity was a constant feature. It invariably showed up in his monastic conferences. Such assertions as "Rilke is the most fantastic poet of this century," were certain to be followed within three, or at most four, weeks, by: "Of course, you can't put much stock in Rilke's approach to things. He was awfully limited when it came to . . ."

This pattern was one of the few predictable things about his style. It caused no end of trouble to some of the younger monks. It is leading some writers even now to misinterpret certain of his most personal and basic positions with regard to his monastic vocation and his relations to the social problems of the age.

Returning to the citation from the preface to the Japanese translation of his autobiography, if Merton's assertion about the monastery as his home and his counter-assertion that the monastery "is not a place where I am rooted and established on earth" is a good instance of his dialectical temper, it is still more significant for the theme it alludes to of the transformed-self and the whole question of identity which, as I have already stated, became crucial to Fr. Louis in his last years.

Concern with personal identity and with its relation to the ultimate Self and with the process of transformation whereby the conscious ego undergoes a metamorphosis in which it yields its place, disappearing into the state of fully realized consciousness, all had prominence in Merton's spiritual life from the beginnings of his monastic vocation. He opens his autobiography with a description of his identity in a vocabulary that is at once biblical and psychological:

On the last day of January, 1915, under the sign of the Water Bearer, in a year of a great war, and down in the shadow of some French mountains on the borders of Spain, I came into the world. Free by nature, in the image of God, I was nevertheless the prisoner of my own violence and my own selfishness, in the image of the world into which I was born. That world was the picture of Hell, full of men like myself, loving God and yet hating Him; born to love Him, living instead in fear and hopeless self-contradictory hungers. (*The Seven Storey Mountain*, p. 3)

Repeatedly throughout his monastic life concern with the question of identity returns in diverse situations and under various guises:

By this time I should have been delivered of any problems about my true identity. I had already made my simple profession. And my vows should have divested me of the last shreds of any special identity.

But then there was this shadow, this double, this writer who had followed me into the cloister. . . .

Nobody seems to understand that one of us has got to die.

Sometimes I am mortally afraid. There are the days when there seems to be nothing left of my vocation—my contemplative vocation—but a few ashes. And everybody calmly tells me: "Writing is your vocation." (*Ibid.*, p. 410)

Later on as Master of Novices at Gethsemani he touches once more on the theme of identity: "In the choir are the young monks, patient, serene, with very clear eyes, thin, reflective, gentle, confused. For fifteen years I have given them classes. Thus they become more confused. Today perhaps I tell them of Eliot's *Little Gidding*, analyzing the first movement of the poem ('Midwinter spring is its own season'). They will listen with attention thinking some other person is talking to them about some other poem" ("Day of a Stranger").

He goes on to analyze his attitude concerning identity in a style that is deliberately paradoxical, protesting against the suggestion that he has an identity identifiable by anybody:

For instance: the fact that I have a *name*. Does this mean that I am expected to produce a certain habitual presence which corresponds to this name? Do I have to secrete a curious fidelity to these two syllables? A disliked but conscious and unfailing Mertonism? I protest. If there is such a thing then surely it begins with a kind of dumb and walleyed re-

fusal to be Merton. Let's forget that whole subject. It is irrelevant. In an age where there is much talk about "being
yourself" I reserve to myself the right to forget about it,
since in any case there is very little chance of my being anybody else. Rather it seems to me that when one is too intent on "being himself" he runs the risk of impersonating
a shadow.

. . . Doubtless I am a stranger to others. (*Ibid.*)

At one point too he speaks of his function as a spiritual
writer in terms of identity and the self, and in a beautiful,
moving passage he reveals, implicitly, how his non-identity
was leading him to a greater identification, by intuitive sympathy, with all men, especially his readers: "Therefore most
honorable reader, it is not as an author that I would speak to
you, not as a story teller, not as a philosopher, not as a friend
only; I seek to speak to you, in some way, as your own self.
Who can tell what this may mean? I myself do not know.
But if you listen, things will be said that are perhaps not written in this book. And this will be due not to me but to One
who lives and speaks in us both" (Author's Preface to the
Japanese edition, p. 13).

But for Fr. Louis the spiritual life of the monk was never
merely a private affair. He was at one with the monastic tradition in appreciating the role of the monk within the
Church and within human society. Entering the monastery
for him was not an escape from the human condition and the
problems and sufferings of mankind. Rather, as he wrote, the
monastic life represents a positive position in relation to man;
it is basically affirmative of the absolute value of human life,
of the person who is transcendent. This view of man leads to
a refusal to become involved in those actions and practices of
modern society which degrade man. A monastic vocation is
therefore both affirmation and protest: "To adopt a life that
is essentially non-assertive, non-violent, a life of humility and
peace is in itself a statement of one's position. . . . It is my
intention to make my entire life a rejection of, a protest
against the crimes and injustices of war and political tyranny. . . ."

More recently he brought together the themes of monastic life as those of protest and of spiritual identity: "Only the man who has fully attained his own spiritual identity can live without the need to kill, and without the need of a doctrine that permits him to do so with good conscience. . . . it is the solitary person (whether in the city or the desert) who does mankind the inestimable favor of reminding it of its true capacity for maturity, liberty and peace" (*Raids on the Unspeakable*, p. 22).

The idea expressed here of the man of full spiritual identity as the solitary man who lives, in one form or other, on the margin of society, and yet is benefactor of that society, became more important as the climate of protest rose in this country and in the world at large. In his Calcutta Conference, October, 1968, he developed at length his thought about this central idea: "In speaking for monks, I am really speaking for a very strange kind of person, a marginal person, because the monk in the modern world is no longer just an established person with an established place in society. We realize very keenly in America today that the monk is essentially outside of all establishments. [The monk is a man] who withdraws deliberately to the margin of society with a view to deepening fundamental human experience."

Spiritual maturity, liberty, solitude, the deepening of human experience, protest against infringements of man's dignity—all these terms are constants in the Merton glossary. All are elements, present from the beginning and closely bound together, in his monastic spirituality. One of the more forceful expressions he has given to this complex vision is in the lengthy poem called *Elias: Variations on a Theme*. The last stanza sums up the whole.

> Under the blunt pine
> Elias becomes his own geography
> (Supposing geography to be necessary at all),
> Elias becomes his own wild bird, with God in the center,
> His own wide field which nobody owns,

His own pattern, surrounding the Spirit
By which he is himself surrounded:

For the free man's road has neither beginning nor end.

THE TRUE MAN OF NO TITLE:
HOMECOMING AS ULTIMATE TRANSFORMATION

Gregory of Nyssa was one of Fr. Louis's favorite authors. He was attracted to the Greek Fathers generally, especially Maximus the Confessor, Pseudo-Denis, and Gregory Palamas, for all were great mystical theologians. But Gregory of Nyssa offered a special interest to him and one reason for it was his teaching on *epektesis*. The idea of *epektesis* is that the perfect spiritual man is not the one who has "arrived" at a high degree of moral perfection and contemplative knowledge of God. Rather, he is the man who, having attained a high measure presses on in pursuit of still purer, more vital experience of God's light and truth. The perfect man is the man who is ever moving forward, deeper into the mystery of God. Heaven itself, in this view, consists in an eternal progress into the love and light and life of God, where each fulfillment contains in itself the impulse to further exploration.

All along Fr. Louis had been interested in Oriental thought, art, and religion. He had made a rudimentary study of the Eastern world not too long before coming to the monastery, and he never lost his interest in it. However, in the last decade of his life he began to concentrate more seriously on Eastern studies and techniques of meditation. Meantime he had dedicated himself seriously to the study of the Latin and then, later, the Greek Fathers, where he found a mentality congenial to his own contemplative interests. He got back to his Greek, which he had not used for a long time, and I recall seeing him, in the interval after Vigils, at his desk reading the Philokalia in the new Greek edition, put out in 1957.

There is not space here to indicate how these patristic readings influenced his ideas on the identity question, on the life of meditation, and on the nature of man's dignity and personality. Profoundly influential, however, they were, and he continued with a lively interest in these writings. (I have a card here before me found in his breviary just after his death, written in Greek by his own hand, citing a passage from John Karpathios: "Let us present our spirit naked to God. . . .")

As he became more deeply involved in Oriental readings and established contact with various Hindu, Buddhist, and Sufi spiritual leaders the question of identity, always so prominent in his thought, tended to take the form of deepening involvement in the mystery of the Transcendent Self.

In his meditations and personal development the various aspects of transformation of the Self assumed increasing significance. He wrote increasingly of the Eastern religions. Furthermore, he came to feel with growing conviction that on every plane of life, from political to mystical, the situation of the world called for a dialogue between the East and West. He saw his role in this movement as interpreting the monastic and mystical traditions of each to the other. He had been active in ecumenism among various Christian denominations for a long time; long before the Council there were such meetings at Gethsemani initiated by Merton. But now it was non-Christian ecumenism that offered greater appeal to his irenic spirit.

The mystical, contemplative experience of these Eastern traditions with the techniques of meditation that, over the ages, had been so profoundly and richly explored and elaborated seemed to him to offer opportunities for his own further development and, as a result of his own experience, hopefully, he would be able better to communicate with Eastern monks. He was convinced that Western monks in general had a great deal to learn from these traditions precisely in the area of the contemplative experience. Thus his trip to the East was a movement in his own *epektesis*, a stage in his self-realization. He would make use of Eastern techniques of meditation to deepen his consciousness, in faith, of the mystery of Christ, as he said at the very end of his Bangkok address. In *Zen and the Birds of Appetite* he spoke of what this process of self-realization and the Transcendent Self meant for a Christian. It was the person as "found and actualized in union with Christ" (pp. 74–75).

When his plane took off from San Francisco for Asia, Fr. Louis wrote in his Asian journal that the beads of condensed moisture streaming down the cabin window as the great jet sharply rose over the Pacific seemed to him as tears of joy and expectation. Would he find on this journey the Great Solution (that is to say, full realization of the transcendent self)? It was this expectation that had caused him to fairly "bounce with joy" at the prospect of visiting the East.

His various conferences and talks in India and Thailand were filled with these themes. He emphasized the marginal nature of monastic life in the present day West and, somewhat whimsically (for if closely questioned he would have qualified himself) identified himself in one talk with the hippies. He saw the monk as one with all true protestors against injustice and inhumanity, and with all who suffer unjustly from the "establishment." "The marginal person, the monk, the displaced person, the prisoner, all these people live in the presence of death which calls into question the meaning of life."

His final statement, made the day of his death in Bangkok, deals explicitly with the question of identity, speaking of the *identity crisis* of the monk who finds himself in the revolutionary social world of today. Total inner transformation, the birth of the new man, is what defines the aims and practices of monastic life. He describes his vision of true humanism and the role of the monk in the revolutionary modern world:

The monk belongs to the world but the world belongs to him insofar as he has dedicated himself totally to liberation from it, in order to liberate it. . . . If you once penetrate by detachment and purity of heart to the inner secret of the ground of one's ordinary experience, you attain to a liberty which nobody can touch. . . . I as a monk, and I think you as monks, can agree that we believe this to be the deepest and most essential thing in our lives, and because we believe this we have given ourselves to the kind of lives we have adopted. (Bangkok Conference)

Not long before, he had spoken of the importance of fidelity to this vocation which called a man to live in solitude and to contribute to the world's welfare and progress, not by direct activity so much as by purifying the heart. That this was his own way, his own vocation, remained his deep and constant conviction. He knew that among men true communication is at its best not a matter of action but of communion, and is without words. This communication "is beyond words and it is beyond speech and it is beyond concepts. Not that we discover a new unity, we discover an older unity. My dear brothers, we are already one, but we imagine that we are not. And what we have to recover is our original unity. What we have to be is what we are" (Calcutta Conference).

When death came to Fr. Louis it came suddenly but not as a surprise. He had often written of death in his books and shortly before leaving for Asia spoke of it still more frequently. All along he lived out his monastic life in the presence of life-beyond-death and thus, at the same time, with a peculiar consciousness of death which as he said in Calcutta, "calls into question the meaning of life." His lightheartedness in the face of death was the result of a profound commitment, in hope, to faith in the Resurrection, not to any lack of awareness of its negations. Is not death disarmed before faith in Christ and childlike confidence in his blessed mother's intercession?

Take time to tremble lest you come without reflection
(says death) because I come as quick as intuition . . .
Yet all my power is conquered by a child's "Hail Mary" . . .
                                        ("Death")

Above all, is death not a new beginning, a movement in the final transformation where God becomes the center of my circle whose circumference is everywhere and where, lost, every step carries me deeper into freedom, and every unknown landmark awakens recognition of a primal identity, and thought and desire turn the eyes of my being, in love, toward the face of Christ?

Not long before leaving for the East, before his fatal accident, Fr. Louis spoke of his desire to remain a member of his community of Gethsemani till death, and expressed his wish to be buried at the abbey, in whose cemetery, under the great cedars, he had so often meditated in the shadow of the monastic church, and had seen visions of hope for a world whose sin and suffering he knew so well. He rests there now, beneath the trees that for him were living symbols of a transformed world and of the power of the cross of Christ.

But look: the valleys shine with promises
And every burning morning is a prophecy of Christ
Coming to raise and vindicate
Even our sorry flesh.

Then will your graves, Gethsemani, give up their angels
Return them to their souls to learn
The songs and attitudes of glory.
Then will creation rise again like gold
Clean, from the furnace of your litanies:
The beasts and trees shall share your resurrection,
    And a new world be born from these green tombs.
                    ("The Trappist Cemetery—Gethsemani")

THÉRÈSE LENTFOEHR

THE SOLITARY

In one of the shorter poems of Thomas Merton—a poem which he later had lettered on the jacket of *The Solitary Life*, a monograph printed on the handpress of his late friend, Victor Hammer—he begins: "If you seek a heavenly light, I, Solitude, am your professor."* With ever so slight a change of words one might amend it to read: "If you seek Solitude/I, Thomas Merton, am your professor." For, if Thomas Merton could be said to have had a persistent theme — one that exercised him from his beginning years in the monastery, and with renewed emphasis in the last years, the years in the hermitage; a subject that he not only wrote about but *lived* in an unusual "experiment," as he called it (for it was new to the American Cistercian monasteries)—it was *solitude*. As a result, since Merton and through him, we have come to a much more comprehensive understanding of the term, to a fuller and richer meaning that may cause surprise for the rich ambience with which it surrounds the traditional

---

* This poem first appeared on the dust-jacket of *The Solitary Life*, printed by Victor Hammer at his press in Lexington, Kentucky, in 1960: The Stamperia del Santuccio Press. It was later published in *Emblems of a Season of Fury*. Over the years Victor Hammer and his wife, Carolyn Reading Hammer, had become very dear friends of Father Merton, and had printed a number of limited editions of Merton's manuscripts, including *Prometheus*, *Hagia Sophia*, *What Ought I to Do?* as well as several broadsides, *The Ox Mountain Parable*, *The Unquiet Conscience*, etc. Since Merton's death, Mrs. Hammer has supervised the printing of *Early Poems* and the Pasternak/Merton correspondence entitled *Six Letters*; the latter was published under the imprint of the University of Kentucky King Library Press—EDITOR.

definition. This extended meaning which Merton made accessible not only posits solitude within the preserve of every man, but makes it a necessity for him by reason of the fact that he is a man.

The need for solitude is related to the natural cycle of man's need for rest, leisure, something more than work—a natural need expressed in the Sabbath rest. In this context the contemplative life is a far more civilized pattern than any the technological age can offer, for work is a *means* not an end.

"Christians are emerging from an era of individualistic piety," said Merton. With a new realization of their oneness as "the people of God," whose rich, communal overtones blend into a "solidarity in love, work, and responsibility," there has been a corresponding emphasis on the meaning of *person*. This has resulted in "a new awareness of the seriousness of *solitude*, not simply as an expression of man's existential plight, but as a Christian value, a challenge, and even as a vocation" (*Contemplation in a World of Action*, pp. 237 ff).

That this preoccupation with the *person* and *solitude* is not new, Merton was well aware, as he points to the Christian existentialists who were deeply concerned with this aspect of personal life and cites Gabriel Marcel with what he says of man in "mass society." But perhaps more to the point here is a quotation from Marcel's disciple, Emmanuel Mounier, in his book *Personalism*, where he speaks of a dialectic of exchange between man and nature—of "exchange and ascension": "If the person is from the beginning, a movement towards others (being-towards), from another point of view it reveals something else, no less distinctive, the pulsation of a secret life which is the ceaseless spring of its productivity" (Emmanuel Mounier, *Personalism* [New York: Grove Press, 1952], p. 33).

This "inner life" or "inwardness" is *not* the opposite of communication, but rather its complement. In the tumult of living one must in a sense "break away" (from environment), recollect oneself, reflect, in order to "reconstitute and re-

unite oneself in one's own center." This re-integration of the
personality, this refreshment of powers, this re-assembling of
forces, which can be had variously—in the contemplation of
the natural beauty of the countryside, in art, music, play and
recreation, and in prayer—shall we say a "wordless prayer"?—
creates an inner solitude filled with God's presence, a solitude
in which one feels himself a part of the unity of creation. Solitude and contemplation are grounded in the human personality and its needs; some more than others have this great
need to be alone; they *must* be alone, and it is in this
aloneness that creativity is found. Thomas Merton the poet,
the artist, was aware of this as only the most sensitive of men
are aware of it—the contemplative vision which can be had
only in solitude, the vision of a child. Here one recalls Rilke's
remark in *Letters to a Young Poet*, "Only one thing is necessary: solitude. To withdraw into oneself and not to meet anyone for hours—that is what we must arrive at. To be alone as
a child is alone when grownups come and go." Merton emphasized this point in a rather late article called "Notes on
the Future of Monasticism" in which he speaks of a solitude
whose measure and degree will vary from person to person:
"I am not defending a phony 'hermit-mystique,' but some of
us *have to be alone* to be ourselves. Call it privacy if you like.
But we have thinking to do and work to do which demands a
certain silence and aloneness. We need time to do our job of
meditation and creation" (*Contemplation in a World of Action*, pp. 218–225).

Through the years that I have known Thomas Merton,
both in his writings and in his friendship, it has been a
deeply moving experience to follow the development of his
thought on solitude. The elements of his mature thought
were obviously latent from the beginning, as was bound to be
the case because of the inevitable linkage of solitude with
contemplation. And even after Thomas Merton had obtained
an enviable amount of solitude by permission to reside in the
hermitage, his thought far from remaining static took on a
startlingly strong social, ecumenical, and universal flavor. By
the time he set out on his Asian trip, it was with a desire to

learn more of and to share the contemplative wisdom gained in his own special solitude. For years his solitude had reached out to the solitudes of the East with its rich contemplative heritage; now it was time and the occasion for spirit to meet spirit.

EARLY PROBINGS

The Seven Storey Mountain, and his early journals, *The Sign of Jonas,* clearly show that Thomas Merton was an exceptional person—one who, by reason of his special temperament and gifts, could be very much his own company. And yet, by some strange paradox this was joined to an exuberance of spirit that expressed itself in a warm, disarming friendliness and affection. These two strains in him were held in some precarious balance. To this was added that extreme sensitivity of the creative artist who, under the impulse and inspiration of his gift of "making," is capable of that sudden detachment when time and space fall away and one lives in a world of spirit.

He writes of summers in Europe—France, Germany, Italy—when he would break away from the cities and take long walks alone in the countryside, perfectly content to be his own companion. At St. Bonaventure's he had a favorite walk in the woods, later named for him, and on the wooded knobs around the abbey of Gethsemani he trudged in all weathers. In his first years as a monk he tells of his own "private board walk" behind the old horse-barn where, when his heart was full, he would sing snatches of Stravinsky and plainsong. It is general knowledge that at this time the call to solitude was so insistent that it constituted a real temptation to leave the Trappists and join the Carthusians, and it was only after a number of years that he finally came to peace with himself, seeing that he should remain where he was and trust God to provide him with whatever solitude was needful.

Solitude then, with its multiple proliferations of extension and meaning—and in Merton's case some of these are quite specific—would seem to be the key for understanding him and his writings.

In the Prologue to *The Sign of Jonas*, speaking of the five vows taken by Cistercians at the time of their profession, namely, poverty, chastity, obedience, stability, and the conversion of manners, Merton has a special remark on the vow of stability: "But for me, the vow of stability has been the belly of the whale. I have always felt a great attraction to the life of perfect solitude. It is an attraction I shall probably never entirely lose" (*The Sign of Jonas*, p. 10).

His own attraction drew him one way, while God seemed to point another—a dilemma that placed him in a perfect "Jonas context," which became, connotatively, the main theme of the book. In fact, as the flyleaf of the manuscript of the second notebook indicates, it was first called *The Whale and the Ivy*. For he, like Jonas, who traveled away from Nineveh where God wanted him to go, was shipwrecked and thrown overboard and, as Merton remarked, "it was the whale that took him where he should have gone in the first place." So too "I am traveling toward my destiny in the belly of a paradox."

Throughout this book his early desire of solitude is apparent; the entries are far too numerous to mention. "Pray me into solitude," he begs. This word, and its adjective, "solitary," appear so frequently that they have the flavor of an obsession. One must, however, remember that Merton's suffering point, if we may call it so, at this time was his need for quiet for prayer—the contemplative's great need and desire which, as he soon discovered, is difficult to come by in the context of a large and flourishing monastery. For a temperament such as his one can easily imagine that rigid structure rubbed hard, though he strove to observe his rule with the strictest detail. When still a young monk he once sent me his daily schedule, which he had minutely written out with each moment of the day accounted for, and which he had pasted on the wall of the vault where he worked. The most frequently repeated line is "prayer in the chapel," where he would actually flee to be alone with God. These were the years of *The Sign of Jonas* and *Thoughts in Solitude*. In the former, in an entry dated January 12, 1947, speaking of the simple architecture of such Cistercian abbey churches as Sénanque or Fontenay, he ventured a remark on the hermit life, saying that such monasteries "could only house a community of cenobites. A monastery of hermits is necessarily so clumsy that it can only be an architectural monster." And he quickly adds, "However, I agree that one hermitage for one hermit stands a good chance of being beautiful." At this point he little thought that one day one hermitage for one special hermit, would be not only beautiful, but known internationally, and from it some of the important spiritual literature of our day would come—the home of a hermit-monk who *loved the world*, and was deeply moved by its suffering and injustices. Some of the passages in the book are near prophetic: "I ought to know by now, that God uses everything that happens as a means to lead me into solitude." And at the close of this entry: "Today I seemed to be very much assured that solitude is indeed His will for me and that it is truly God Who is calling me into the desert. But this desert is not necessarily a geographical one. It is a solitude of heart in which created joys are consumed and reborn in God" (*ibid.*, p. 52).

For his contemplative spirit the long hours in choir were difficult: "I was once again irritated with the choir and with the work I am doing and with everything in general and went back to the old refrain about being a hermit" (*ibid.*, p. 56).

We find a like eremitic flavor in some of the poems of this period. However, in the office of Master of Scholastics assigned him after his ordination he discovered a new solitude. In one of the most moving passages of the book he speaks of meeting them (his scholastics) in his own solitude.

The best of them, and the ones to whom I feel closest, are also the most solitary. . . . All this experience replaces my theories of solitude. I do not need a hermitage, because I have found one where I least expected it. It was when I knew my brothers less well that my thoughts were more involved in them. Now that I know them better, I can see something of the depths of solitude which are in every human person, but which most men do not know how to lay open either to themselves or to others or to God. (*Ibid.*, pp. 336–37)

In mid-July of 1955 (in spirit we always observed the feast of Carmel together) he sent me his long poem "Elias: Variations on a Theme," saying, "it is the most appropriate thing I can think of for the feast of Carmel—Elias, zealous for the Lord God of Hosts, and felled by despair under the juniper tree, and fighting his way to Horeb. . . . I suppose there will be a book for this, with other poems around it, in a short while." (Letter, July 12, 1955). It appeared in *The Strange Islands* (1956). John Eudes Bamberger in "The Cistercian" in the Merton Memorial issue of *Continuum*, speaks of this poem as "one of the more forceful expressions he has given to this complex vision" of monastic spirituality which combined "spiritual maturity, liberty, solitude, the deepening of human experience, protest against infringements of man's dignity." That the poem held a central position in Merton's thought is evident from these lines in a letter of August 6, 1955:

> You like Elias. It makes a sort of turning point in my life. . . . What I am hoping for now is to find some real solitude. Things at least seem to be shaping up to provide me with some, after all these years. God works slowly, and I am not the most prudent man in the world, so I think it is a very good thing that He works slowly. . . . Yet now that I think of it, things are moving faster than one would think . . . but there is some hope of my becoming at least a quasi-hermit.

His reference was to the fire-lookout post on a high hill near the Abbey, of which he had been given charge—an assignment with which he was delighted. He had made a private retreat, the poem "Elias" being more or less its summation, "the conviction of a solitary vocation of some sort. Because solitary vocations do not fit into neat categories. And neither do I." All he knew at the time was that it would be of "some sort," and what he called the "big development" came after he stopped trying to fit himself into "too neat a category—'carthusian' for instance."

WITH THE NOVICES

But there was another category into which, unexpectedly, he was to be fitted. "I thought I was headed for the fire tower and silence," he wrote on October 22, "and I find I am moving in the other direction." The abbatial election at the Genesee took the Gethsemani Novice Master, and Thomas Merton was chosen to replace him. "I have the disadvantage of a strong attraction to the woods and to solitude, and I suppose that would spoil everything if my desires were ever fulfilled." But there was a bright note, "I shall still be in charge of the forest and take the novices out to fell trees, and to plant in the spring."

In 1958 *Thoughts in Solitude* appeared, the content of which actually anteceded its publication by some five years and was strongly influenced by Merton's reading of Max Picard's *World of Silence*. In it Merton says that "when solitude was a problem, I had no solitude. When it ceased to be a problem I found I already possessed it." But already in the book's introduction, written at the time of its publication, one notes the influence of the existential philosophers as he speaks of man's inalienable solitude and interior freedom:

> In an age when totalitarianism has striven, in every way to devaluate and degrade the human person, we hope it is right to demand a hearing for any and every sane reaction in favor of man's inalienable solitude and his interior freedom. The murderous din of our materialism cannot be allowed to silence the independent voices which will never cease to speak: whether they be the voices of Christian Saints, or the voices of Oriental sages like Lao-Tse or the Zen Masters, or the voices of men like Thoreau or Martin Buber, or Max Picard. (*Thoughts in Solitude*, p. 12.)

Merton insists that persons in society are not mechanical units; their existence depends on their inviolable personal solitude, "and to be a person implies responsibility and freedom, and both these imply a certain interior solitude." He closes the preface by remarking that what he is about to say concerning solitude is not just "a recipe for hermits. It has a bearing on the whole future of man and of his world."

As will be immediately noted, Merton's concept of solitude had already taken on a universal note as he related it to existential man, his interior solitude, freedom, and the gift of himself to society.

In April of 1958 I received a manuscript of what he called the "original-original"—the first draft notes of the book, and some three years later what might have been called the "original-original original,"—a manuscript of fifty-four sheets, tightly written (as only Merton could tightly write), composed at the time of *Thoughts in Solitude*. Of the manuscript he said: "It consists of notes and things written about the time of *Thoughts in Solitude*. They are personal, on the whole, and a bit contemplative I hope. You might enjoy piecing bits of it together when you have nothing else to do. If you find anything you think worth while, let me know. But I am not thinking of making a book out of them" (letter, May 10, 1961).

At this time he was deeply impressed by his readings in Max Picard's *The World of Silence*, and among other quotations which he noted down was "in silence man is as he was before the creation of language." In one place in this manuscript Merton relates solitude to various virtues, and especially to what he called "poverty of the spirit," reminiscent of the poem he composed about this time called "When in the soul of the serene disciple . . ." with its first stanza.

> When in the soul of the serene disciple
> With no more Fathers to imitate
> Poverty has become a success,
> It is a small thing to say the roof is gone,
> He has not even a house.
> (*The Strange Islands*, p. 86.)

In another place in the same manuscript he writes: "in a totalitarian world, there is need before all else, of hermits—her-

mits that are saints. I would say that perhaps we needed soli-
taries even more than martyrs."

Thomas Merton's preoccupation with solitude was not always met with understanding. In 1955 he sent me an offprint
of an article he had written for *Témoignages*, a magazine of
the Benedictines of Pierre-Qui-Vire, France. On its deep
olive cover he had written, "This is rare, controversial, has
not appeared in English, only in French and Italian." However, by 1960 he was prepared to speak out fearlessly and
eloquently for the solitary life, and in "Notes for a Philosophy
of Solitude" in *Disputed Questions*, gave his ripened thought
on the subject to that date. Speaking of this essay he wrote:
"I think it says a lot of things I want to say, but naturally, it
will be discussed, 'disputed.' It already has been much
so. . . . The censors did not like the bit on solitude. As you
say, this is most truly myself—you have a keen eye to see it,
you must know me well. It is what I most want to say, almost all I really deeply want to say. Everything else just
points to this" (letter, September 12, 1960).

Even before its publication in *Disputed Questions*, fifty
copies of the second half of the essay, specifically on the hermit life, had been privately printed by Victor Hammer at the
Stamperia del Santuccio Press in Lexington, Kentucky, and
was titled *The Solitary Life* (*pro manuscripto*). I was surprised when Merton later wrote: "About the little privately
printed thing on solitude, please do *not* mention it in print
anywhere. It is strictly a private printing, of only fifty copies,
and as it stands it was not censored, in fact, it is a version to
which one censor objected. Hence it is printed only as a manuscript and is not considered to be in general circulation. It
does not even 'exist' officially. It must not begin to do so"
(*ibid.*).

The hermit life was already close to his heart, and it will
be remembered that in 1960 he had published *The Wisdom
of the Desert*, selected sayings of the Desert Fathers, a portion of which had previously appeared in *Harper's Bazaar*. In
my copy he wrote the following inscription: "These silent

old men—you have already met them—one does not grow tired of their conversations."

A PHILOSOPHY OF SOLITUDE

"Notes for a Philosophy of Solitude" is perhaps Merton's strongest and most extended writing on the subject to that time. Later there was to be the preface to the Japanese translation of *Thoughts in Solitude,* and an article called "Christian Solitude," both of which contained a description of his own "experiment" of the hermit life. In a footnote to the essay he explains that the "solitary" of whom he speaks "is never necessarily a 'monk' (juridically) at all. He may well be a layman, and of the sort most remote from cloistered life, like Thoreau or Emily Dickinson." He begins the study by asking, "Why write about solitude in the first place?" and answers: "Certainly not in order to preach it, to exhort people to become solitary. What could be more absurd? Those who are to become solitary are, as a rule, solitary already . . . all men are solitary. Only most of them are so averse to being alone, or to feeling alone, that they do everything they can to forget their solitude" (*Disputed Questions,* p. 177). And that by distractions of every sort, and Merton refers to Pascal's *divertissements* "which enable a man to avoid his own company for twenty-four hours a day." His emphasis in the first part of the essay is on "interior solitude," interiority, which one can have in the midst of crowds and every distraction. Such a man, he says, must be responsible for his own inner life, face its mystery (though it be a dark one) and work his lonely way through it "until he discovers that his mystery and the mystery of God merge into one reality—God" in a way that words cannot begin to communicate. Merton cites death as the example: "when a man dies, he dies alone." Rereading this passage now, one recalls the tragedy of Bangkok, and the monk who died suddenly—not only interiorly alone, as each man must, but literally alone. At the same time, each one must *live* alone, a fact that is sometimes difficult to face. The true solitary does not need to leave society, but to *transcend* it. "He seeks a spiritual and simple

oneness in himself which, when it is found, paradoxically, becomes the oneness of all men—a oneness without separation,
conflict, and schism. . . . His solitude is neither an argument, an accusation, a reproach or a sermon. It is simply itself" (ibid., p. 184).

One called to solitude, Merton insists, realizes, though it
may be confusedly, "that he has entered into a solitude that
is really shared by everyone," and is one with them in the
peril and anguish of their common solitude—a solitude that is
not that of the individual only, but "the radical and essential
solitude of man." Of such a person he says: "When you get
to know him well—which is sometimes possible—you may find
in him not so much a man who seeks solitude as one who has
already found it, or been found by it. His problem then is
not to find what he already has, but to discover what to do
about it" (ibid., p. 189).

In discovering his inner solitude he has simply discovered
what it is to be a man. The last half of the study is devoted
to that special kind of "solitary" who is a "hermit," what
Merton himself became after many years of waiting, though
at the time of this writing it was still some five years or more
away. With keen insight and precision he situates the hermit
in his place in the world, in the Church, and with men. As to
one who has been "found" by solitude, he "falls into the desert the way a ripe fruit falls out of a tree," a desert, he explains, that may well be in the midst of men, as well as far
from them. The "true self" emerges to full maturity in solitude; in fact, without it there can be no maturity.

This concept of full maturity or "final integration" of the
person, which can only be arrived at in some manner of solitude, Merton underscored some years later in an article called
"Final Integration: Toward a Monastic Therapy," published
in Monastic Studies a month before his death. In this he
takes "the state of insight which is final integration" as set in
the context of the Persian psychoanalyst, Reza Arasteh's
study, "Final Integration in the Adult Personality," and carries
it into a Christian and specifically monastic dimension, showing that this must be articulated in more than psychological

terms. If in the past it was the privilege of the few, it is now, because of man's existential crisis, become a need and aspiration of *mankind as a whole*. Citing the language of Sufism used by Doctor Arasteh in describing the breakthrough into final integration—*Fana*, a "loss of self, a real spiritual death," followed by *Baqa*, "a reintegration and a new life on a totally different level," Merton remarks that this process involves "a terrible interior solitude . . . a crisis and an anguish which cannot be analyzed or intellectualized" and requires a solitary fortitude far beyond the ordinary, and, quoting Arasteh, "an act of courage related to the root of all existence. . . . Seen from the viewpoint of monastic tradition, the pattern of disintegration, existential moratorium and reintegration on a higher, universal level, is precisely what the monastic life is meant to provide."* With this Merton was acutely concerned. But the essay must be read in its entirety.

To return to the regard in which Merton held the solitude theme, this may be the place to remark that he was never oversensitive about what critics might say of his books (though he had his share of troubles with monastic censors), but when this criticism touched on his cherished subject of solitude, he could become disturbed. When a certain writer stated that Merton's best work was *No Man Is an Island*, and that he had done nothing good since, he was cut to the quick and wrote: "His perspective is all off. Not that I claim to be doing especially good work, but to pick *No Man Is an Island* which is vague and not characteristic, and overlooking something like the notes on solitude in *Disputed Questions*, which is really what I have to say, shows he does not know who he is dealing with at all. He is not able to discriminate between one thing of mine and another" (letter, February 5, 1961).

Too, the criticism of the Trappist censors hurt him keenly; their attitude toward the essay on solitude in *Disputed Questions* he found absurd. Merton rarely complained. "I wrote an article on solitude and anyone would think it was an ob-

---

* This article was later published in Merton's posthumous volume, *Contemplation in a World of Action.*—EDITOR.

scene novel. . . . I really got in trouble. I rewrote the thing three times, and these rewritings were further developments of an original version written in 1955 or earlier and published only in French and Italian. I never could get that one past the American censors; (the others did not give it a second thought!)" (letter, May 30, 1960).

However, one can, to an extent, understand the sensitivity of the Order on the subject of solitude, or the "solitary life," since the tradition of the cenobitic life was considered the ideal. "It is unpalatable among us," Merton said. But later he apologized for mentioning this, and did so only because he thought I would be amused. But these attitudes of the Trappist censors have changed considerably. Since the second American meeting of the Cistercian abbots of North and South America, held in October, 1964, at Gethsemani, there have been adaptations that allow for the creation of hermitages or *laura*, to one of which the former Abbot of Gethsemani has himself retired, the present Abbot having been a hermit before his election with a hermitage about a mile from that of Thomas Merton. And if, as Merton's writings indicate, his thoughts on solitude steadily evolved, so too did those of his monastic censors, for in Merton's last years he wrote openly and freely of solitude.

THE HERMITAGE

In the fall of 1965, his superiors granted him what he most desired—the solitude of a "modern" hermitage. The chronological history of Merton's becoming a hermit is well known. He had previously been spending more or less time in the cinder-block cabin originally designed for dialogue with ecumenical visitors. I heard of it in a letter of August 15, 1965:

. . . this week I officially begin the hermit life . . . the new novice master is all set to take over, and I am all set to go. . . . It is quite a step, and something that has not been done thus officially in the Order since the Lord knows when, way back in the Middle Ages, when we had a few hermit saints. I hope I will follow in their footsteps (sanely however). Expect to come down to the monastery for Mass and one meal, and will continue to give one conference a week to the novices, serve on private council, etc. So I am not climbing a pillar or being entombed.

Later, except for the weekly conference, Merton remained at the hermitage almost exclusively, even, as he said, "risking my own cooking." In the letters that came from that hermitage there was always high praise of it: "It is fine, and silent—and lonely. I have no questions about this being the kind of life for me, but it is certainly nothing to play with. It is hard. You really have to face yourself, and believe me that is quite grim. But at least it has one consolation: it makes sense" (letter, February 16, 1966).

Serious as this was to him, even before becoming a "full-time" hermit, he took a lot of what he called "good-natured ribbing" about his propensities for solitude. While he was still Novice Master he had sent me what he had called "a classic work of art," which the novices had made for his anniversary. It was a booklet with an artistic watercolor and ink sketch of himself standing before the hermitage. He thought it clever and wrote: "They are not afraid to kid about the hermitage, but I don't have a pipe or that kind of hat either, still less a gun. After all, I am a disciple of non-violence" (letter, September 2, 1963).

It was eventually from this hermitage that his most mature writing continued to come, up to the days of his leaving for Asia, and when one comes into the wide country of his ripened thought one is astounded at its depth, its richness, and its comprehension. Nor was he reluctant to share with others his "experiment." One of the most moving accounts, in which one catches the sheer poetry and prose of his great spiritual adventure, is "Day of a Stranger," originally written in 1965 for a South American publication; it later appeared in the *Hudson Review*. An excerpt follows:

The hermit life is cool. It is a life of low definition in which there is little to decide, in which there are few transactions or none, in which there are no packages delivered. In which I do not bundle up packages and deliver them to myself. It is not intense. There is no give and take of questions and answers, problems and solutions. Problems begin down the hill. Over there under the water tower are the solutions. Here there are woods, foxes. Here there is no need for dark glasses. "Here" does not even warm itself up with references to "there." The hermit life is that cool. (*Hudson Review*, 20 (1967), 211–18.)

However, perhaps Merton's most seasoned thought on solitude is contained in his preface to the Japanese edition of *Thoughts in Solitude*, composed in March and April of 1966, eight years after the book had appeared in English. It was his happy custom to write a new preface to some of the translations of his books, and this was especially true of Japanese translations; this was the time of his growing interest in Zen Buddhism that came to so swift a ripening. In these prefaces he embodied new commentary and new insights of his ever-evolving thought. Later this particular preface was expanded into an article called "Love and Solitude," in which he elaborated no defense but rather let solitude "speak a little and say something for itself." Then the poet and the mystic take over: "No writing on the solitary, meditative dimensions of life can say anything that has not already been said better by the wind in the pine trees. . . . But what can the wind say where there is no hearer? There is then a deeper silence: the silence in which the Hearer is No-Hearer. That deeper silence, must be heard before one can speak truly of solitude." "Who is the No-Hearer?" he asks, and answers that it is the Hearing itself, whose proper climate is solitude, or, better, *is* solitude. He differentiates between solipsism and solitude, contrasting the state of one who has merely isolated himself from others in a false unity of separation, and that of one who has lost himself in order to become *all*, identifying himself with that ground of being in which all being hears and knows itself—a unity which is *Love*. Again he asks: "Is it true to say that one goes into solitude to 'get at the root of existence?' It would be better simply to say that in solitude one *is* at the root. He who is alone, and is conscious of what his solitude means, finds himself simply in the ground of life. He is 'in love.' He is in love with all, with everyone, with everything. He is not surprised at this, and he is able to live with this disconcerting and unexciting reality, which has no explanation. . . . one disappears into Love, in order to 'be Love!'" But solitude is by no means exclusively the province of the professional "solitary" or hermit: "Solitude is not withdrawal from ordinary life. It is not apart from, above, 'better than' ordinary life. It is the very ground of that simple, unpretentious, fully human activity by which we quietly earn our daily living and share our experiences with a few intimate friends. But we must learn to know and accept this ground of our being" (*ibid.*, p. 9).

One might also point up the similarity of this love-dimension (the theological basis of solitude) with Merton's description of "Transcendent Experience," in *Newsletter Review,* later appearing as a chapter in *Zen and the Birds of Appetite.* In this he speaks of an experience of metaphysical or mystical self-transcending, and the experience of God, "the transcendent Absolute," not so much as object, but as subject —"the absolute ground of Being, realized from within Himself and myself the latter lost and 'found' in Him." And he speaks of a self that is "no-self," but by no means an alienated self; rather, a transcendent self, metaphysically distinct from the Self of God, and yet perfectly identified with that Self by love and freedom, so that there appears to be but one Self. He also names it the "illumination of wisdom."

To attain this experience is to penetrate the reality of all that is, to grasp the meaning of one's own existence, to find one's true place in the scheme of things, to relate perfectly to all that is in a relation of identity and love. For "the paradox of solitude is that its true ground is universal love—and true solitude is the undivided unity of love for which there is no number" ("Love and Solitude," p. 2).

In pursuing Thomas Merton's developing thought on the meaning of solitude, in which the hermit life-style presented for him its very refinement, we find that at the beginning of his monastic life it was for his contemplative spirit a mecca

of flight from the tensions and rigidities of the strictly structured life and prayer of the Trappist monk. In this struggle
there was much of the purely personal attraction toward the
eremitical life, for him a *given* by grace and temperament, an
attraction which understandably met with opposition and
under which he suffered greatly. But as he matured in spiritual living, his concept of solitude took on richer definition.
By the time "Notes for a Philosophy of Solitude" appeared in
Disputed Questions (actually, its genesis was in that brief article in *Témoignages*), he was ready to make a first public
stand on the issue which concerned him so deeply. It had
already taken on new dimensions, and he was certain of its
deeper existential meaning involving all men. Solitude was
not only *his* problem, but that of *every man*, in fact, a part
of being a man: "if a man can't be alone he doesn't know
who he is."

Then came the three years of the hermitage—1965–68,
perhaps the most creative of his life, and especially in the extension of his concept of solitude. These were the years of
"The Day of a Stranger," preface to the Japanese edition of
Thoughts in Solitude, "Love and Solitude," and "Christian
Solitude." These not only elucidated and summarized his
fully integrated thought on the subject, but sharply situated
it in the province of every man, so that by the time of *Conjectures of a Guilty Bystander* (completed in manuscript in
1965), he could say in a moving passage (the one entry in
that book specifically listed under "solitude," though it
flavors and illumines the entire text): "Solitude is to be
preserved, not as a luxury, but as a necessity: not for 'perfection' so much as for simple 'survival' in the life God has
given you" (p. 82).

His whole emphasis was on what he called the "gift" of
solitude as not oriented to "strange contemplative powers,"
but to the recovery of one's deep self. "We must be *persons*
who can give ourselves, because we have a self to give." How
can we give Christ, he asks, unless we have found Him, and
how can we find Him, if we cannot find ourselves?

Merton's thought on the dimensions of solitude might best

be concluded by the closing lines of the poem, "Song: If you
seek . . ." quoted at the beginning of this paper:

> For I, Solitude, am thine own Self:
> I Nothingness
> am thy All. I
> Silence
> am thy 'Amen'!

DAVID STEINDL-RAST

MAN OF PRAYER

When I remember my last visit with Thomas Merton I see him standing in the forest, listening to the rain. Much later, when he began to talk, he was not breaking the silence, he was letting it come to word. And he continued to listen. "Talking is not the principal thing," he said.

A handful of men and women searching for ways of renewal in religious life, we had gone to meet him in California as he was leaving for the East, and we had asked him to speak to us on prayer. But he insisted that "nothing that anyone says will be that important. The great thing is prayer. Prayer itself. If you want a life of prayer, the way to get to it is by praying.

"As you know, I have been living as a sort of hermit. And now I have been out of that atmosphere for about three or four weeks, and talking a lot, and I get the feeling that so much talking goes on that is utterly useless. Something has been said perfectly well in five minutes and then you spend the next five hours saying the same thing over and over again. But here you do not have to feel that much needs to be said. We already know a great deal about it all. Now we need to grasp it.

"The most important thing is that we are here, at this place, in a house of prayer. This is probably the best Cistercian monastery in the United States. There is here a true and authentic realization of the Cistercian spirit, an atmosphere of prayer. Enjoy this. Drink it all in. Everything, the redwood forests, the sea, the sky, the waves, the birds, the sea-lions. It is in all this that you will find your answers. Here is where ev-

erything connects." (The idea of "connection" was charged
with mysterious significance for Thomas Merton.)

Three sides of the chapel were concrete-block walls. The
fourth wall, all glass, opened on a small clearing surrounded
by redwood trees, so tall that even this high window limited
the view of the nearby trees to the mammoth columns of
their trunks. The branches above could only be guessed from
the way in which they were filtering shafts of sunlight down
onto the forest floor. Yes, even the natural setting of Our
Lady of the Redwoods provided an atmosphere of prayer, to
say nothing of the women who pray there and of their charismatic abbess. On the day we had listened to the Gospel of
the Great Wedding Feast, flying ants began to swarm all
across the forest clearing just as the communion procession
began, ten thousands of glittering wings in a wedding procession. Everything "connected."

To start where you are and to become aware of the connec-
tions—that was Thomas Merton's approach to prayer. "We
were indoctrinated so much into means and ends," he said,
"that we don't realize that there is a different dimension in
the life of prayer. In technology you have this horizontal
progress, where you must start at one point and move to another and then another. But that is not the way to build a
life of prayer. In prayer we discover what we already have.
You start where you are and you deepen what you already
have, and you realize that you are already there. We already
have everything, but we don't know it and we don't experience it. Everything has been given to us in Christ. All we
need is to experience what we already possess.

"The trouble is, we aren't taking time to do so." The idea
of taking time to experience, to savor, to let life fully come to
itself in us, was a key idea in Thomas Merton's reflections on
prayer. "If we really want prayer, we'll have to give it time.
We must slow down to a human tempo and we'll begin to
have time to listen. And as soon as we listen to what's going
on, things will begin to take shape by themselves. But for this
we have to experience time in a new way.

"One of the best things for me when I went to the hermitage was being attentive to the times of the day: when the birds began to sing, and the deer came out of the morning fog, and the sun came up—while in the monastery, summer or winter, Lauds is at the same hour. The reason why we don't take time is a feeling that we have to keep moving. This is a real sickness. Today time is commodity, and for each one of us time is mortgaged. We experience time as unlimited indebtedness. We are sharecroppers of time. We are theatened by a chain reaction: overwork—overstimulation—overreaction—overcompensation—overkill. And yet, we are not debtors of the flesh (the flesh which is for St. Paul the principle of indebtedness). Christ has freed us.

"We must approach the whole idea of time in a new way. We are free to love. And you must get free from all imaginary claims. We live in the fullness of time. Every moment is God's own good time, his *kairos*. The whole thing boils down to giving ourselves in prayer a chance to realize that we have what we seek. We don't have to rush after it. It is there all the time, and if we give it time it will make itself known to us."

In contrast to the man whose time is mortgaged, the monk is to "feel free to do nothing, without feeling guilty." All this reminded me of Suzuki Roshi, the Buddhist abbot of Tassajara, who had said that a Zen student must learn "to waste time conscientiously." I was not surprised, then, to hear Thomas Merton refer explicitly to Zen in this connection. "This is what the Zen people do. They give a great deal of time to doing whatever they need to do. That's what we have to learn when it comes to prayer. We have to give it time." There is, in all this, a sense of the unfolding of mystery in time, a reverence for gradual growth.

We were sitting in front of a blazing fire when Thomas Merton again took up this theme of growing. "The main theme of time is that of inner growth. It's a theme to which we should all return frequently in prayer. There is a great thing in my life—Christ wants me to grow. Move this around a little bit in meditation. Instead of worrying, where am I going? What kind of resolution should I make? I should simply let this growing unfold in my prayer. I should see what is holding me back from it. What is it? What kind of compromises have I made? Am I substituting activity for growth? (I have often asked myself, is this writing getting in the way? For me writing is so satisfying an activity that it is hard to say.) In someone else it is easier to see this process of growing and to see what hinders it. But when it comes to ourselves, all we can do is try to honestly be ourselves.

"One of the greatest obstacles to your growing is the fear of making a fool of yourself. Any real step forward implies the risk of failure. And the really important steps imply the risk of complete failure. Yet we must make them, trusting in Christ. If I take this step, everything I have done so far might go down the drain. In a situation like that we need a shot of Buddhist mentality. Then we see, down what drain? so what? (So that's perhaps one of the valuable things about this Asian trip.) We have to have the courage to make fools of ourselves, and at the same time be awfully careful not to make fools of ourselves.

"The great temptation is to fear going it alone, wanting to be 'with it' at any cost. But each one of us has to be able to go it alone somehow. You don't want to repudiate the community, but you have to go it alone at times. If the community is made up of a little group of people who always try to support one another, and nobody ever gets out of this little block, nothing happens and all growth is being stifled. This is possibly one of the greatest dangers we face in the future, because we are getting more and more to be that kind of society. We will need those who have the courage to do the opposite of everybody else. If you have this courage you will effect change. Of course they will say, 'this guy is crazy'; but you have to do it.

"We are much too dominated by public opinion. We are always asking, what is someone else going to think about it? There is a whole 'contemplative mystique,' a standard which other people have set up for you. They call you a contemplative or a hermit, and then they demand that you conform to the image they have in mind. But the real contemplative standard is to have no standard, to be just yourself. That's what God is asking of us, to be ourselves. If you are ready to say 'I'm going to do my own thing, it doesn't matter what kind of a press I get,' if you are ready to be yourself, you are not going to fit anybody else's mystique."

He himself certainly didn't. When I saw him for the first time at the Abbey of Gethsemani he was wearing his overalls and I thought he was the milk delivery man. He wasn't going to fit my mystique either. Two other faces came to mind whenever I looked at his features, Dorothy Day and Picasso. When the chapel was getting dark and he bent down to hear confessions, there was more of Dorothy Day. When he read poetry (his own reluctantly, but his friends' poems with relish) there was more of Picasso. Again and again I was amazed to find him at once so totally uninhibited and so perfectly disciplined.

He saw the wrong kind of self-fulfillment as one of our great temptations today. "The wrong idea of personal fulfillment is promoted by commercialism. They try to sell things which no one would buy if he were in his right mind; so, keep him in his wrong mind. There is a kind of self-fulfillment that fulfills nothing but your illusory self. What truly matters is not how to get the most out of life, but how to recollect yourself so that you can fully give yourself." Self-acceptance, sober and realistic, was basic in Thomas Merton's view.

"The desert becomes a paradise when it is accepted as desert. The desert can never be anything but a desert if we are trying to escape it. But once we fully accept it in union with the passion of Christ, it becomes a paradise. This is a great theological point: any attempt to renew the contemplative life is going to have to include this element of sacrifice, uncompromising sacrifice. This breakthrough into what you already have is only accomplished through the complete acceptance of the cross at some point. There is no way around it if we want a valid renewal."

It was with tongue in cheek that he spoke of renewal. "We have been pushing, pushing, pushing. Then came good

Pope John. The door burst open, and now we are falling over each other, rolling down the stairs on the other side of the door. Let's face it, anything is possible now. Really, if you keep within reason you can do anything you want. But people keep pushing like mad on the most unlikely, most unreasonable things, just because there is nothing else left to push on, and they are so used to pushing. We have spent so much time pushing that we have never stopped to figure out what in the world we really want.

"So now, when most anything is possible, we really don't know what we want to do. And so we find all these little contemplative experiments being started, like among the Cistercians. They start and they evaporate. Kids who have come through a traumatic experience, pushing for real contemplative life, are suddenly being told: 'O.K. Here you are, go ahead and do it. Work the whole thing out.' They buy themselves a farm and set themselves up in a farmhouse, and suddenly realize that they either have to do it the old way (which they absolutely refuse to do), or they have to find a better way of their own (which they don't have). Then come the meetings and the dialogues, and it becomes an interminable yak session. And it evaporates.

"Maybe new structures are not that necessary. Perhaps you already do know what you want. I believe that what we want to do is to pray. After all, why did any of us become religious if we didn't want to pray? What do we want, if not to pray? O.K., now, pray. This is the whole doctrine of prayer in the Rule of St. Benedict. It's all summed up in one phrase: 'If a man wants to pray, let him go and pray.' That is all St. Benedict feels it is necessary to say about the subject. He doesn't say, let us go in and start with a little introductory prayer, etc., etc. If you want to pray, pray.

"Now that all the barriers are taken away and the obstacles gone and we find ourselves with the opportunity to do whatever we want, we see the real problem. It is in ourselves. What is wrong with us? What is keeping us back from living lives of prayer? Perhaps we don't really want to pray. This is the thing we have to face. Before this we took it for granted that we were totally dedicated to this desire for prayer. Somebody else was stopping us. The thing that was stopping us was the structure. Now we simply find that maybe a structure helps. If some of the old structure helps, keep it. We don't have to have this mania for throwing out structures simply because they are structures. What we have to do is to discover what is useful to us. We can then discard structures that don't help, and keep structures that do help. And if it turns out that something medieval helps, keep it. Whether it is medieval or not doesn't matter. What does matter is that it helps you become yourself, that it helps you live a life of prayer."

Finding your true self and living a life of prayer were not two things for Thomas Merton, but one. For him structures and institutions had no value in themselves, and yet he saw their great importance in helping people find themselves in prayer. Again and again he came back to this point: "It's all a matter of rethinking the identity of the institution so that everything is oriented to people. The institution must serve the development of the individual person. And once you've got fully developed people, they can do anything. What count are people and their vocations, not structures and ideas. Let us make room for idiosyncrasies. The danger is that the institution becomes an end in itself. What we need are person-centered communities, not institution-centered ones. This is the direction in which renewal must move."

There is a remarkable development taking place within all active orders. Many of their most dedicated members are discovering the great importance of the contemplative dimension of their religious life. In fact it was in this context that our little group was approaching Thomas Merton with questions about prayer. He was keenly interested in this so-called House of Prayer Movement, and considered it possibly the most promising movement within the Church today. The name has come into use because the most noticeable phenomenon is the establishing of Houses of Prayer within active orders (although these houses differ greatly from one another).

"Call it anything but House of Prayer," Thomas Merton pleaded. "Make it a House of Renewal. If you think you know what it ought to be like, you are already on the wrong track. It ought to be a forum for rethinking the very foundations of your community life. Let's not structure it to the point of obstructing its purpose, which is to give a chance to people for a personal breakthrough to greater maturity. It should be a place for all creative efforts of contemplatives. A house of spiritual research. Maybe prayer itself has to be renewed before we can have houses of prayer."

Much that was discussed referred specifically to the situation of active orders. But Thomas Merton felt that "the House of Prayer question is becoming a focal point for the re-examination and recovery of the identity of all religious life, that of the monks included. What we need in our houses of prayer are leaders who will help individuals to mature. The real function of the abbot is to be purely and simply a spiritual father who leads you to the point where you can go on your own, and then throws you out to do just that. He doesn't hold on to you any longer. But our institutions have always an inclination to turn this completely upside down. The institution calls you to something and then holds on to you for life, and you can't move beyond. It gets you to a certain point of usefulness, makes you a cog in the wheel of the communal machine, and then that's the way you are for life. You are not supposed to develop. Think of the lay brothers.

"I think it would be useful if we had a little more knowledge of how this sort of thing happens, say in the business world. In business and management people are intensely worried today and research teams are set up to study the fact that it's so easy for everybody just to fall into a neat little slot and never really develop. They are worried about the immense amount of money spent on keeping all these useless slots operating for their own sake. That's not my field. But someone ought to draw out the lines of this as far as religious life is concerned.

"Who are the people who need a House of Prayer? Mature religious who have served their communities well and who can foresee nothing else in the future but more and more official positions—a dead end to their religious vocation, which after all is the life of prayer. Of course these are the most valuable members of the community. But the supreme reward in a religious community should be that a man or a woman be set free for what they most desire. We'll just have to work this out in our communities.

"In the Greek monasteries this is foreseen. You have three steps: first, many years without commitment; then commitment and duties; finally (the great habit or *schema*) ultimate commitment and complete relief from duties. In our case people are relieved from duties when they go to the infirmary. Can't we produce people who are still physically strong and yet free to follow the lead of the Spirit? A certain amount of eccentricity will have to be taken in stride here."

The smile with which he said this, and his witty criticism of his own idiosyncrasies, made it clear that he realized that eccentricity is not without risk. But neither is prayer. "It's a risky thing to pray, and the danger is that our very prayers get between God and us. The great thing in prayer is not to pray, but to go directly to God. If saying your prayers is an obstacle to prayer, cut it out. Let Jesus pray. Thank God Jesus is praying. Forget yourself. Enter into the prayer of Jesus. Let him pray in you. (The Jesus Prayer is the best way to forget that you are praying. But don't take away from weak people the crutches they need.)

"The best way to pray is: stop. Let prayer pray within you, whether you know it or not. This means a deep awareness of our true inner identity. It implies a life of faith, but also of doubt. You can't have faith without doubt. Give up the business of suppressing doubt. Doubt and faith are two sides of the same thing. Faith will grow out of doubt, the real doubt. We don't pray right because we evade doubt. And we evade it by regularity and by activism. It is in these two ways that we create a false identity, and these are also the two ways by which we justify the self-perpetuation of our institutions.

"But the point is that we need not justify ourselves. By grace we are Christ. Our relationship with God is that of

Christ to the Father in the Holy Spirit. A Christian is no longer under judgment. He need not justify himself. I must remember both that I am not condemned, yet worthy of condemnation. How can I live the message of Christian newness in these final days? I am not called to gather merit, but to go all over the world taking away people's debts. (This is not the prerogative of a priestly caste.) We need a theology of liberation instead of an official debt machine. I belong entirely to Christ. There is no self to justify."

There were so many points of contact with Zen Buddhist teaching in all this that I couldn't help asking whether he thought he could have come to these insights if he had never come across Zen. "I'm not sure," he answered pensively, "but I don't think so. I see no contradiction between Buddhism and Christianity. The future of Zen is in the West. I intend to become as good a Buddhist as I can."

And yet, Thomas Merton's Christian faith wasn't watered down to the point where it would become compatible with most anything. It was throbbing with life. This came out most clearly in little personal remarks, for example in what he said about so traditional a theme as prayer of intercession. "We are not rainmakers, but Christians. In our dealings with God he is free and so are we. It's simply a need for me to express my love by praying for my friends; it's like embracing them. If you love another person, it's God's love being realized. One and the same love is reaching your friend through you, and you through your friend."

"But isn't there still an implicit dualism in all this?" I asked. His answer was, "Really there isn't, and yet there is. You have to see your will and God's will dualistically for a long time. You have to experience duality for a long time until you see it's not there. In this respect I am a Hindu. Ramakrishna has the solution. Don't consider dualistic prayer on a lower level. The lower is higher. There are no levels. Any moment you can break through to the underlying unity which is God's gift in Christ. In the end, Praise praises. Thanksgiving gives thanks. Jesus prays. Openness is all." He was ready to go to Bangkok.

PATRICK RYAN

TWO POEMS

MERTON

Seventy men
Held the city
Rigid and tight

Someone ran out
Into the desert night

Every now and then
He would throw a handful of sand
Into the wind

A MAN: T.M.

Prophets never age

They live too strong
To prolong
Their days

Pure heart
Friend
Your words remain
To test our heart

You, word,
Will never age

JEAN LECLERCQ

THE EVOLVING MONK

"UNLESS A GRAIN OF WHEAT FALLS INTO THE GROUND AND
DIES . . ."

What was true of Christ is also true of his disciples: something in us, something of ourselves, must die for the fruit to be born; and the greater the degree of death, the greater will be the rebirth and the fruit. Recently I started rereading the letters that I had had from Thomas Merton. From the very first one of those I had kept, dated 1950, he expressed his hope of seeing formed in his country's monasteries men capable of "cultivating in their souls the grain that is the word of God" and of bearing fruit in the field of spiritual theology. He himself never ceased to work toward this goal. He never really saw the result of his efforts; but, for example, under the title of *Cistercian Publications*, a project is taking shape, with the general plan of which he was acquainted, and of which the first volume is a posthumously published book of his own (*Contemplative Prayer*, 1969).

I am writing this as I am about to leave for the first convention, in Korea, of the Union of Asiatic Monasteries. When Merton was taken from us, in December, 1968, at the beginning of the Meeting of the Monks of Asia, at Bangkok, we all made a promise to God, in the presence of his body and in communion with his spirit, to carry on the work he loved and to which he had dedicated his efforts earlier than any one of us—the creation of an Asiatic Christian monasticism, beginning in the country where he died. He only saw the start of our work. Today, a small group of Christian monks who have chosen to become a part of the cultural and religious fabric of Asia has come into being in Thailand. And within a few days, representatives of monasticism from five Asian countries will remember Merton and his presence among them and try to find ways of becoming at the same time more truly Christian, more completely monks, more wholly Asiatic.

Throughout his life as a Trappist, Merton tried to overcome what he called, in one of his letters, an excess of "rigidity" in his own Order's structure. He wanted a spiritual and institutional renewal which he knew would meet with some resistance, and in his last days one felt that he was almost hoping against hope. But only a few months after his death, one of his students was entrusted with an important office which had to do with the renewal of the entire Cistercian Order.

For fifteen years he wrote and taught and worked in every way that he could to try to insure that monks in the communal life, when they reached maturity, would bear fruit in the solitary life. He was stunned by the lack of comprehension of those who thought that "the hermit's life was inhuman." By patience and obedience, yet always faithful to what he clearly recognized as a call from God, he won approval to live as a hermit himself, and it was easy to see that he became not only more a monk, but also more human: closer to men, to all men, more universal. Before he died, he saw his former abbot become a hermit and his community elect as successor a student whom Merton himself had trained and who was living, as he did, in a hermitage not far from the monastery. And now, from the North to the South Pacific, from Oregon to Santiago de Chile, and elsewhere throughout the world, I have encountered Trappists who are living as hermits to everyone's satisfaction.

One could go on citing areas where Merton's fruitfulness was equal to his sacrifice. These few examples suffice to show that his work was linked to his experience: he wrote with his entire being, he lived and died for what he was teaching, he suffered for the truth of his message.

THE MISSION

There were in him, not two men—for few personalities
have been as well integrated as his—but two spheres of activity: that of the writer—what he called with self-deprecating
irony, "being an author"—and that of the close friend. He excelled in making the reader feel that he was close to him,
that he even identified with him. That was the whole secret
of his appeal. I remember, one day in England, asking a
young man who had become a Christian through reading
The Seven Storey Mountain why this book moved him so
much. "I felt," he answered, "that this story was my story: I
followed Thomas Merton's path and I reached the end of it,
just as he did." When one knew Merton personally, one realized that his friendship was far richer and deeper than would
have appeared even from the warmth of his writing.

When his spiritual journey is traced in the light of all the
texts and all the memories he left behind, it will be seen, I
think, that the first years of his monastic life were used for an
intense scrutiny of history. Not that he engaged in what he
himself called, in the 1950 letter to which I have already referred, "a mass of futile research," but he read, studied, tried
to understand the greatest possible number of witnesses to
the spiritual life in which he himself was being formed, and
which he believed himself called upon to teach. He knew he
had a mission: he would speak of "the job Providence has
given to me." He had a tremendous capacity for enjoying
every sign of beauty, every spark of truth, but it was by no
means for his own pleasure that he read the early writers: he
believed he could understand tradition only through immersing himself in the knowledge of the past. His study of history
was his preparation for the present.

Even before I met him at Gethsemani, I had been
watching his development through his letters. I shared, at a
distance, in his successive enthusiasms—which both stimulated and amused his fellow monks—for the Desert Fathers,
the Greek Fathers and their vocabulary, for Clement, Origen,
the Alexandrians, for Diadochus of Photike, for Cassian, and

in the Middle Ages for Grimlaic, Aelred, Adam of Perseigne, for St. Bernard in particular, and then for Blessed Paul Giustiniani. He asked incessant questions about them. His intuition enabled him to go straight to the essence of a passage and to make it his own.

Yet, at the same time, he was acutely aware of everything which was gestating or was already happening within the Church: the first foundations of "simple monasteries" in France, following World War II; the changing pattern of several monastic orders; the expansion of monasticism. When I began my trips to Morocco, and then into Black Africa, and later to Asia, he would always ask, not about details, but about basic problems, the direction in which things were moving, the hopes and the aims. He never refused to write a note or send a book to some unknown monk who owed his vocation to Merton's writing; to someone poor or sick whom I had met and who was too shy to write to him. Then came the Vatican Council and his close interest in the successive schemas of the Decree of the Renewal of Religious Life and particularly in how it was going to treat of monks.

The problem of eremitism arose very early in his correspondence. For him it was not just a topic for academic discussion: it was a matter of life and death. But the quality of his scholarship is clearly evident in the fact that as he pursued his vocation he never bypassed historical or theological points: he was rooted in the Church and in its tradition. Someday we shall learn of the struggles which arose from his longing for the life of solitude, until finally he was given the solution which brought him peace. When one realizes that he had also to contend with critics who would have preferred a less strident message, one can fully grasp the fact that his writing was supported and nourished by personal and often painful experience.

Only two years before his death, in a letter dated November, 1966, in which he thanked me for having publicly defended him against those whom he described as "these nice 'defenders of the faith,'" he described himself as someone "whom most people don't know what to make of." He added two things which sum up the two sides of his vocation: "that which is the basis of my solitude . . ." and "that which helps me evaluate my own life and my position in the Church."

Isolation, misunderstanding, but always the conviction of a mission, a sense of totality: always the two aspects of the same paradox. The position of a servant who is not above the Master: "If the grain of wheat does not die, it will bear no fruit."

THE MESSAGE

If Merton was convinced that he had a mission it was because he knew that he had a message. A message is not necessarily a scholarly lecture—and when Merton spoke from a platform he was not at his best. He was not dealing, after all, with abstract knowledge, timeless science, a course which could be given again and again, unchanged, each year. According to its etymology, which is the same as that of mission, a message is always composed of truths sent (*missus*) to a person, a group, a period in time, to satisfy an expectation and sometimes to answer a call for help. Those who receive it may not even have understood their need, but even before they recognize it and are able to express it in words, they have been looking for that message and hoping that someone will come to help them and that God will send them a messenger. A message is, therefore, something prophetic, mobile, running, even flying—St. Bernard used the word *praevolare*—to fulfill man's hopes. They take it for granted that its author, or messenger, has had a glimpse of the solution of their problem; prophecy implies the gift of anticipation. But each time the pace quickens, each time that anyone sees farther than the "man of the actual moment," as Kierkegaard put it, there is bound to be opposition. A message is something for which one must suffer and occasionally die. Certainly a message cannot remain a personal possession: definitely it must be "delivered."

As I reread Merton's letters, remembering his other works, his ideas about the message recur to me. He expressed his thoughts on so many subjects, from the arts to politics, and touched all aspects of religious life. Yet, at the heart of everything he said was his vocation, his monastic experience. He saw everything through a monk's eyes. This was both his limitation and his strength: a limitation because, after all, monastic life is not the totality of the Church, or of society; other points of view are also valid. A strength, because he was a man of single purpose, a lone warrior. He persevered until the final moment, and now the message has been delivered, has been decoded, and has begun to bear fruit.

What originally made Merton's message contemporary, and still keeps it so, is what might be called its dynamism, in the original meaning of the word, which conveys a force in motion. He was not concerned with a "definitive work," a scholarly tome, needing no further commentary, but with a number of "essays," trials, thrusts, breakthroughs moving beyond the fragile present, which others are now trying to consolidate in order to preserve the message and increase its life.

Thomas Merton was the man Christianity needed in a time of transition which began, not with Vatican II, but with World War II. Earlier than others, he had seen, he had known without a doubt that—in monasticism as well as in everything else—many things would change. One might even say everything—except the essential, except for Him Who is not a thing, and the primordial encounter made with Him in love. Merton understood that it was necessary to reinforce the foundations if the whole structure were not to collapse. All the details, the outward observances, ideas even, all these "things," could change; but the union of man with God in Jesus Christ, through his Church, for the salvation of the world would continue to be a living reality. Faith need not be shaken, hope need not be disappointed, love need not be lessened.

It is the dual orientation which one sees throughout his monastic work and it is that which gives it its unity. On the one hand there is the protest against the exaggerated worth attributed to the historic observances of monasticism, its so-called traditional practices and ideas, which in many cases go

back no further than the nineteenth century, or at the very
most to the seventeenth; and, on the other hand, there is an
increased emphasis on spiritual experience which is reached
in prayer and love: "union with God" is not the whole of the
mystery, because the experience is at the same time communion with men. Solitude in which there is no other activity at
all becomes, for Merton, the symbol of this absolute, ultimate, and inexhaustible encounter with God and with hu-
manity. More and more in his writing, the idea, too easily labeled ambiguous because of its appeal to "feelings," of
"intimacy with God," gives way to the idea of objective,
effective union with the Word manifested in and by Jesus
Christ, far beyond all sensation, in the humble recognition of
one's self as a sinner, in the mysterious allegiance to Him
Who identified Himself with our condition, in order to trans-
form it. Nothing occurs, nothing happens, and yet everything
is given, received, shared, given back by God to man in many
ways, through the written word, through conversation,
through the example of a smile, of joy, and the message becomes more and more specific, simple in its form, more and
more direct and perhaps even shocking, but always more apt
to leap over the barricades, to push back the frontiers.

A message presupposes a language which changes as the
message evolves. From the serious, almost pedantic, tone of
The Ascent to Truth to the all but goliardic irony of the
journal of art and poetry, *Monks Pond*, which Merton edited
and sent his friends in the late sixties, what progress there
had been! In the crucible of patience and contradiction, all
had been purified, simplified, and calmed; yet everything is
more vigorous and the vehemence has sometimes almost a
note of violence. Some people even feared that he might go
too far in his championship of freedom, which might explain
how it was possible for someone to make the completely incredible remark I heard about his death: "It was really the
Trappists who liquidated him. . . ." But his abbot, his
brother monks, his friends are all convinced that God called
him back, and that in him patience and impatience are rec-

onciled, thanks to a power which gives a peace far beyond our frail security.

PUSHING BACK THE FRONTIERS

I have not written thus far without emotion, in this Soviet jet flying swiftly over Siberia, carrying me to Asia. I took along on this journey only two Merton mimeographed texts: the prefaces he wrote for the Japanese editions of *The Seven Storey Mountain* and *Seeds of Contemplation*. Flying over this Marxist world which interested him so much—he was to draw parallels between it and monasticism in his last speech on the very day of his death—and going to Japan, where so many friends had waited for him, I cannot help thinking about the image he had of himself during these last years, about the way in which he saw his own development.

In his letters, his writings, the conferences he gave at Gethsemani on the Christian and the World, the talks he gave in the United States and in Asia on his last trip, he seemed to be more and more preoccupied with the relationship which the Church and Christians, monasticism and monks could and should have with the world. He meditated deeply on the major problems of contemporary culture: Marxism and Neo-Marxism, mass media and communication between men, technology and urbanization. He read and evaluated recent and contemporary writers such as Faulkner, Camus, Koestler, Garaudy, Hromodka and Marcuse. He was interested in the new sociology, saw its impact on the monasticism of the present-day society, in the encounter between East and West at every level. But his point of view remained essentially religious: he did not consider that any area could be indifferent or foreign to the affinity which exists between God and man.

In his later monastic writing, he often returned to Buddhism. In an essay in 1967 on "Marcel and Buddha" he chose to stress the idea that the emphasis on presence to the world was common to Buddhist teaching as well as to Marcel's. He took exception to the purely negative concept—all too popular in the West—of "nirvana," just as he spoke out against a Christian contemplation which was an escape or a vacuum. All must end in vitality, joy, love—and that is communion. At the same time, in the last talks he gave in India and Ceylon, he was careful always to stress and appreciate what was common to Christian and Far Eastern monasticism: this common factor, above and beyond doctrine and practices, he saw as an "experience" that was both a deeper enrichment and a transcendence. It is in the very center of himself where man encounters God that Merton saw the possibility of a religious communion between the disciples of Christ and the followers of other schools of spiritual thought. In his writings on the spiritual tradition of the Far East, especially on Zen Buddhism, Japanese and other scholars have a right to criticize him for excessive optimism. But for a Christian of the West to adopt this confident attitude was, really, in Merton's case, a manifestation of charity. For there was growing in him, more and more, a search for the essential which is love.

The final stage of his own growth was already apparent in what he revealed of himself to his Japanese readers, some of whom he imagined would not have been formed in Christian tradition. "Twenty years ago," he says, in the new preface to *The Seven Storey Mountain*, "I left the world. But since that time, I have learned—I believe—to look upon the world with more compassion. . . ." He is very definite in saying that his separation from the world did not separate him from men: he found himself identifying more and more with all men. In the beautiful profession of faith in which he affirms his loyalty to what he was, to what he did, and to what he wrote in his youth, the key words of his vocabulary—liberation, the beyond, All—could have been expressed by the religious of the Far East, but for Merton, in Christian terminology, those words mean "to live in Christ," and "in the Spirit." In order to be "in the All" he had to become, not nothing, not a zero, but "nothing," "no thing"; to become a person completely in communion with all others in Christ, and this state is not achieved without sacrifice.

The first thing he had to sacrifice was his reputation: Merton used to smile at the legends that were always going around, all of which tended to discredit him. He did not refute them, he did not complain, yet one felt that the seed had already died in him: soon it would bear fruit. He wanted to make his whole existence an affirmation of peace, of nonviolence, a silent protest against any form of tyranny, against every compromise of Christianity with the secular world and, at the same time, to encourage everything good, beautiful, pure, free in the world and in man. And in doing so, he firmly intended to carry on the protest of the fourth-century monks against the temptation to dominate, to which even for men of faith, power—even Christian power—inevitably leads.

It is always the monk in Merton that has the last word. In 1965, in the Japanese preface to *Seeds of Contemplation*, he faces, in the very first lines, the problem of contemplation. But since Japan is fast becoming a leader in the field of technology, it is the reconciliation of technology and religious experience that claims his attention. How acquire this "inner peace," so little encouraged in the modern man's life of activism, science, machinery, the drive to acquire power and proficiency? In his answer, Merton makes use of a vocabulary that is perfectly acceptable to Oriental contemplatives. He speaks of the "way" and the "wisdom" which help to reduce the divisiveness in us, and thus around us and in the world, and permits us to reach the experience of inner unity, which is the noblest effort man can make for his own good and for the good of all men.

In this connection, Merton offers a formula which gives us the key to his own spiritual progress, to his own "advancement" throughout his last years: "Thus, far from wishing to abandon this way, the author seeks only to travel further and further along it. . . ." Always the same concern with pushing back frontiers, with throwing out anything that might cause disunity. He will come them, traveler as he is, to a meeting place with other pilgrims walking in other traditions and he will know that he is close to them: "The author of this book can say that he feels himself much closer to the Zen monks of ancient Japan than to the busy and impatient men of the West. . . ." The mission of the contemplative, no matter what doctrine he professes, is to work for unity, for peace. Once Merton has stated his common ideal, he can emphasize the distinctive points of his program as a Christian: to become one in all in the Incarnate Word of whom St. John said, "The true light that enlightens every man was coming into the world. . . . In him was life, and the life was the light of men. The light shines in the darkness. . . ."

It is impossible to grasp the whole of Merton's monastic thinking, unless one realizes how far this line of thought would lead him and how far it is right for us, too, to be guided by him. Little by little, today, in the midst of great technological advances, churches and religions are rediscovering their contemplative values. Even before the Pan-Indian Synod of the Church, held in Bangalore in 1969, where the fact that Catholicism appeared to be merely a "way of works" was sharply contradicted, Merton, in his preface to the Japanese edition of *Seeds of Contemplation* pleaded for Catholicism in Asia to manifest "the hidden element of contemplation in Christianity." One sees that he is deeply influenced by his reading in Buddhist literature and, at the same time, faithful to the Cistercian tradition which he had studied so long. He comments on the "unity of spirit" of which St. Paul spoke, in a way that reminds one of St. Bernard's commentary; he seems to be inspired by a saying of William of St. Thierry—"love itself is knowledge"—to show the unity that exists between the two. He argues explicitly from "the tradition of early monasticism." And, at the end, since he had started out with the idea of "the way," he gives the Biblical quotation: did not Christ say, "I am the way, the truth and the life?"

And here I would like to call attention to the construction, which in much of Merton's work is a great deal more disciplined than one would think at first glance from the apparent detours around the subtleties of a fine point, and a style that is poetic and paradoxical. He liked always to come back to the place from which he had started, to restate the theme upon which he had played his free variations. For always he was led back to the same central point: to the same Love, to the God he encountered in Jesus Christ through the gift of the spirit.

I am not giving in to an ingenuous, admiring expression of friendship when I rank Merton with the Fathers of the Early Church and those of the Middle Ages. Not only, as do all Christians, did he live the same mystery as they did, but he lives it and expresses it in the same way. His humanism explains why his message, as did theirs, has found so great an audience. Just as they drew from the culture of their own times in order to make it a part of their inner experience, so did Merton work in our times toward bringing "the good news" to the world, less by converting individuals than by Christianizing cultures. Not that he always stated, any more than the great Fathers, definitive, irrefutable truths; not that he avoided all exaggeration, all error, or was always precise. Nothing would more offend his memory than to read his work uncritically or without personal opinions. But at least he has shown—especially to monks—an orientation, a "way," given a direction for a renewal both free and profound. As he wrote in the letter in which he accepted the invitation to speak at the Congress in Bangkok where he was to die, the great problem for monasticism today "is not survival, but prophecy."

THE SPIRITUAL WRITER

On December 1, 1968, I received a tightly written kodachrome postcard of the Himalayas (Kachenjunga from Mall Road) postmarked Darjeeling, India, and signed "Tom Merton." On it he spoke enthusiastically of his sojourn in the mountains as "a great experience," "I am going to Ceylon and Indonesia," he said, "and expect to see many more interesting people." (He had already had several conferences with the Dalai Lama.) In the late afternoon of December 10, a telegram arrived from the Abbot of Gethsemani announcing Father Merton's sudden death in Bangkok. Of this the whole world now knows.

That his last written words to me were of "mountains" seemed singularly fitting for one born in the Pyrenees, who lived his last years in a hermitage on a high wooded hill in Nelson County, Kentucky, and now—the Himalayas, the Far East, where he went to saturate himself in its contemplative heritage, and to give of his own. But more significant to me at the moment was the symbolism of mountains as the high places of prayer and solitude, a solitude which Thomas Merton had cherished within him from his first years as a Trappist Monk—"My heart consents to nothing but God and solitude" (letter, May 6, 1950). If there is one subject he wrote about in letters again and again, and on the rare occasions when we spoke together—to say nothing of its being a key theme in all his writing—it was the subject of solitude. For Thomas Merton was no ordinary man—though the characteristic that first impressed one on meeting him, and even after long years of knowing him, was a disarming simplicity, transparent of the charism of a man of profound interiority, and "the freedom of the children of God." One might say that by temperament as well as grace he was shaped for solitude and contemplation. He was one of the merriest of men, and one of the most serious. His humor was spontaneous, his conversation of "infinite variety." An artist in more than words, and a sensitive musician, it should occasion no surprise that he had a special resonance for the inner life of the spirit, a heritage which he generously shared with all who knew him either personally, or through his writings. Already in 1951 he had said, "It is really a kind of necessity in the spiritual life to be able to share things of the spirit with other souls—and to do it directly too" (letter, July 7, 1951). And this he did with a world of readers.

Since this paper was to be fashioned more in the manner of a "personal reflection," than a heavily documented study, my sources are primarily Merton's own writings, and the privilege of a friendship of twenty years that was deep and constant. In this context I have attempted to trace the intellectual and spiritual climate of his thought and its development through his early writings as a young monk to its final synthesis in the depth, breadth, and varied scope of his last writings—from *The Seven Storey Mountain* (1948) to his latest published work, *Zen and the Birds of Appetite* (1968). Though every line of his writing on any theme is vibrant with searching insight and spiritual vision, I shall refer mainly to his explicitly theological and religious books.

The seed of such a harvest is sown in early spring. It is general knowledge that from his first years as a monk Thomas Merton was asked by his abbot to translate from the French (in my copy of *La Muntanya Dels Set Cercles* Merton had written, "This is Catalan—in a way my 'native' language") certain small treatises on Cistercian spirituality, notably Chautard's *The Soul of the Apostolate* (1946), in which he contributed a biographical note and *The Spirit of Simplicity* (1948), with notes and commentary. He also wrote the text for *Cistercian Contemplatives* (1947), an illustrated book of Cistercian life, and *Gethsemani Magnificat* (1949) the centenary volume of the Abbey. The translations of the first two books listed were published under the pseudonym "A Cistercian Monk of Our Lady of Gethsemani," the last two anonymously. At this same time a series of the lives of Cistercian saints was projected, the manuscripts of two of them, *Exile Ends in Glory* (1948), the life of a Trappistine in Japan, and *What Are These Wounds?* (1950), the biography of a Cistercian mystic, St. Lutgarde of Aywieres, both to be published anonymously, had already been completed before the publication of *The Seven Storey Mountain*. However after the last book's unprecedented success one can sympathize with the publisher's demand that the hitherto unnamed "Cistercian Monk" who had written these books should be identified. Merton pleaded against it—these were written he told me "right after my novitiate when I thought I knew everything." Nor was he given the manuscripts back for correction as he had requested. His disappointment resulted in my receiving a prepublication copy from the author with witty annotations and hilarious comments penciled in on many of the pages. The books sold reasonably well, however—for Merton's name was magic.

The impact of *The Seven Storey Mountain* has become a legend. Upon the scaffolding of his life story Merton fashioned an edifice of spiritual vision, rarely come upon in our day. He had searched for his true identity, and having found it in Christ, turned his whole being to God. Though still so young in monastic life—a bare seven years when the book was published—he had pierced to the essence of what it means to be a Christian and to the authentic spirit of the Trappist-Cistercian life that he was later to elaborate in numerous writings. The electric success of his book was embarrassing. "My life can never consist in the noise that surrounds the externalization of *The Seven Storey Mountain*, and no matter what happens outside the walls of Gethsemani, I want to be a nobody inside it" (letter, December 27, 1948). Try as he might, as the whole world knows, his wish never came true. "My ambition is to be the most insignificant person in this house," an ambition which he called "consciously selfish" since in being insignificant he would be left alone for God. In certain mysterious ways this *did* come true.

In the spring of 1949, when *Seeds of Contemplation* came off the presses, it met with a prodigious audience, and may yet prove, if not his most enduring, his most popular book. Here was a man who could unabashedly speak of God and of his closeness to Him, sharing with his readers his own experience—an experience that would find a *rapport* in the heart of Everyman. In the interval between the completion of the manuscript and the book's publication, Thomas Merton was already engaged in another work into which he poured his whole spirit with an enthusiasm which was dynamic. In fact, over the years I have never known him so excited over and dedicated to a book in progress; it was a book he was *living* as well as *writing*. First called *The Cloud and the Fire*, and later *The School of the Spirit*, the rough and crowded outline notes for the various chapters attest to its author's precise and scholarly thinking on a subject that had been occupying his mind for a long time. He speaks of it in *The Sign of Jonas* and tells of his difficulty in getting it moving. "I have in mind something that needs to be done some day: the dogmatic essentials of mystical theology, based on tradition and delivered in the context and atmosphere of Scripture and the Liturgy." On January 18, 1949, he wrote apropos of some exchanges we had had on the subject:

> The point you raise about the part played by natural temperament in disposing a soul for contemplation is something I must investigate, especially since I have embarked on the perhaps presumptuous task of writing a kind of theological study of the contemplative life. If you come across anything that will give me further leads in that direction, I would be grateful for the hint. The question of temperament will come into a chapter in which I will try to navigate the stormy waters of "the contemplative vocation" without being shot by the Dominicans or torpedoed by the Jesuits.

There was little to be found, but I copied out passages from

Maréchal, Fargas, Scaramelli, and various others, including the brief footnote quote from Maritain in Tanquerey's *Spiritual Life* which had made us curious in the first place. He was grateful for what he called the "supernatural papers" and added, "the problem is one that interests me, definitely. It is rather a hot one, and I will take care not to get mixed up in it if I can help it" (letter, August 29, 1949). He had many plans for the book and spoke of some eight hundred pages of jottings in various notebooks that he would draw from and organize.

However, later he remarked: ". . . You worry about my writing. I have been publishing far too much and it is time to be quiet for a little. I still have in mind those jobs on St. Aelred and St. Bernard and I do not mean to drop the *School of the Spirit* entirely. Only to take it up again, from a more thoroughly Scriptural and Patristic viewpoint later on" (letter, January 7, 1950). A year later he wrote that the book he had been trying to bind together in a unity "finally split up into two that can be easier finished than that one. This will content the publisher and save the author a few headaches" (letter, January 8, 1951).

The portion of the book that dealt with the doctrine of St. John of the Cross resulted in *The Ascent to Truth*, a carefully structured and brilliant introduction to, and explication of, the writings of the Carmelite saint—a book into which Merton had sieved his ripened and keen theological insight. It has been said that had he written nothing else but this volume he could be accorded a permanent place among the theologians of our day. However, as Merton's theological vision became more acute he had second thoughts about the book, and seven years later in a preface to the French edition, *La Montée vers la Lumière*, dated "All Saints, 1957," he remarks that were he to deal with the same subject today ("and I probably would not") he would approach it quite differently:

For one thing, the psychological aspects of the study would have to be completed by discussion of man's unconscious drives and their possible intervention in the life of prayer. On the other hand I would prefer to draw more upon Scripture and the Fathers and to concern myself a little less with scholasticism which is not the true intellectual climate for a monk. In a word, the book would be quite different from what it is.

One might note here that the translations of Thomas Merton's books into numerous languages gave him opportunity for comment and correction, also in the prefaces which he wrote for many of them, and especially in later years, for translations into the Oriental languages, Chinese, Japanese, Korean, and Vietnamese. "I wonder who will read this in Vietnam today!" he wrote on the flyleaf of my copy of *Hat Giông Chiêm Niêm* (*Seeds of Contemplation*) (1966).

Already in January, 1949, a providential "happening" occurred which fit in perfectly with the monk Merton. He was given the rare book vault as a work room, where he sat surrounded by medieval manuscripts of St. Bernard, and missals, and antiphoners centuries old. Nothing could have made him happier; he referred to it over and over again in his letters: "It is simply wonderful. It is a miracle that I do any work at all. The constant temptation is to sit still and taste the beautiful silence" (letter, January 18, 1949). For all the contemporaneity of his genius there was a "desert" quality about him, as he wrote with special affection of "the cave where I work." In a sense it was his first "hermitage." From his constant references to it over the years the vault grew on me, and as we walked across the courtyard toward the Trappist cemetery on the funeral day, Brother Patrick pointed out to me the window of that "cave where I work" which had been so dear to Thomas Merton. This solitude in the companionship of dusty tomes of the Fathers, undoubtedly had much to do with the rapid ripening and maturing of his mind. But actually, he had acquired a taste for and wide acquaintance with their writings even earlier.

In two small notebooks he had used at Columbia (on whose right-hand pages were class notes on Jacobean Drama and Posterior Analytics) already as a novice he had begun to fill all empty reverse pages with copious Latin texts notably from St. Bernard, Aelred of Rievaulx, William of St. Thierry, and St. John of the Cross, and even a squibble from De Rancé. These texts are most frequently followed by his reaction and personal comment, and sometimes by a spontaneous prayer. It was thus early that he became saturated with the wisdom of saints and scholars, which found a ready response in his own heart.

Not too long after his ordination to the priesthood—of which he wrote, ". . . at last I have found the place in the universe that has been destined for me. . . . I feel as if I had at last awakened to discover my true name and my true identity, as if I had never before been a complete person" (letter, June 2, 1949)—he was given a teaching assignment. "Did you know I got a job teaching? Seventy students, novices and young professed. Course for all of them called Orientation in the Contemplative Life, and for some of them called Mystical Theology. Busy" (letter, February 25, 1950). Of his preparation he remarked that he was "building up from the ground—trying to develop a spiritual theology that suits a contemplative monastery! And one which gives the proper place to the Fathers and especially to our Cistercians." On May 21 he was named Master of Scholastics, which entailed almost entirely spiritual direction. "I have nothing at all against being spiritual director, in fact, I quite like it; but every moment of it makes me wish I lived alone in the woods" (letter, July 7, 1951).

Relevant to his teaching duties Thomas Merton began a series of so-called Orientation Notes in areas of monastic spirituality and theological study, designed as a text for his classes. In this I was privileged to be of some little help to him. These "Monastic Orientation Notes," as they were called, which ran to six series, were mimeographed and bound, but were never published, although freely circulated among the monasteries of his order. Interpolated between the first and second series was an "Introduction to Cistercian Theology," not a systematic course, he insisted, but one designed to show ". . . that such a subject really exists, and that the

Cistercian Fathers really had a 'doctrine' as well as a 'spirit' distinctly their own." In this he outlined the main Bernardian theses, with special attention to the relation of knowledge and love in Cistercian ideas of contemplation. For this Merton had been eminently prepared. To these "Orientation Notes" he frequently appended a section of miscellaneous conferences, random notes, or short homilies on a wide-ranging variety of subjects, such as "St. Thomas on Affability," "The Virtue of Study," "T. S. Eliot's 'Christmas Sermon' from *Murder in the Cathedral*," "Blood-Letting (Red Cross)," "Who Are You? (the U.C.L.A. Test)," a poem of Hopkins, or remarks on one or another of his favorites, such as the hermit Charbel Makhlouf or Simone Weil. About this same time he was teaching a course in Scripture with concentration on St. Paul, which turned out to be "practically a course on Christian liberty which has taught me how much the Christian must struggle to keep his integrity in situations where falsity and formalism mask as religion. Our integrity in Christ is not a luxury; it is an obligation, and it is as great as our humility" (letter, July 10, 1954). Any definitive appraisal of Thomas Merton's writing must take into account his savoring and deep study of the great spiritual writers of Christendom.

After destroying a Journal he had been keeping in the novitiate—actually, seven salvaged pages of poems and spiritual notations remain—he took it up again in 1946. First called (in the notebooks) *The Whale and the Ivy*, it became *The Sign of Jonas*, one of Thomas Merton's most popular and best loved books. Actually, it is more than a book; it is an experience. In a review in *Renascence* I recall situating it in the second of the two attitudes of spirit present in man, as described by Maritain—namely the *imprecatory* (as distinguished from the *sapiential* wherein man searches for causes, and his detachment from self is ordered to the knowledge of being) which is ordered to the saving of one's uniqueness. It is in this attitude of dramatic singularity that the action of *The Sign of Jonas* takes place—the attitude of Jacob battling the angel. No doubt one of the reasons for the book's popularity is its protagonist's "strange wrestling with God" which in some form or other finds a response in every human being. Here is no *persona*, no façade—in fact, Merton has never seen fit to use one in any of his personal writings. He gives himself to us as he is, and we are with him as he lives his daily life with its difficulties, joys, and silences. Here in his delightful informality we are made aware of a certain personal and unique ambience that his abbot in Merton's funeral homily to the monks so aptly described as "a younger Brother, even a boyish Brother, one who could have lived a hundred years without growing old." The Abbot also referred to his "secret prayer" that "gave the inner life to all he said and wrote," and which is more than hinted at—between the lines—on every page of *Jonas*, a text freely flavored with its author's characteristic humor and *esprit*, and transparent of a man of high spiritual gift and purpose. This, one of the most popular of his books, closes with an epilogue which is a prose-poem, "The Fire Watch," dated July 4, 1952. Almost immediately the book was translated into numerous languages, and as early as 1955 he sent me a Danish translation, *Jonas Tegnet*, with which he was particularly happy. One cannot believe that this highly pleasing book, perhaps more than any other, met with unusual difficulties along the way. At one point the Abbot, knowing that I had typed out the greater portion of the Journal from the original holograph, wrote asking my opinion on the prudence of a young Trappist monk's publishing a personal Journal. There is no need for me to give my answer. There were of course the foreseen difficulties with censors, and Merton humbly agreed that there was much wisdom in their decisions. "The book shows quite frankly that I am not much of a religious—a truth which I have no desire to conceal, and it also gives a clear insight into various problems" (letter, November 6, 1952). But since matters had already gone too far with printing and publicizing, it was deemed advisable to let it finally be published. "It is still a big question mark in my mind, that book," he wrote. "Maybe a big mistake" (letter, January 20, 1953). But his readers felt far otherwise.

Thomas Merton was a humble man, open and ready to receive suggestion and correction. In the summer of 1950 while preparing the second edition of *Seeds of Contemplation* "with a few emendations," and learning that the Jesuit theologian Augustine Ellard, whom I knew, was giving a summer course at Marquette, Merton requested that I ask if he had any remark to make on the book, saying that he would value his opinion highly. Father Ellard had a few suggestions, mainly in the area of "probable opinions" which he felt should be stated as such. Merton was deeply grateful, and commented, "I hope to gain some of his wisdom as I go on" (letter, August 28, 1950).

Already at this time he was deeply engrossed in finishing a short book on the Psalter, an expansion of articles first published in *Orate Frates* (*Worship*) which became *Bread in the Wilderness*. This book too, as he told me, went through some of the "weirdest vicissitudes," the manuscript (of which there was only one), "a mosaic of bits and pieces," all but getting lost in process—and much more. However, it finally turned out to be a handsome book, designed by Alvin Lustig, and enhanced by photographs of *Le Dévot Christ*, the startling wood-carved crucifix of Perpignan. (Actually, Merton himself was to have done the original illustrations, and had completed several interesting sketches of Old Testament prophets, and an *Ecce Homo.*) *Bread in the Wilderness* was another Merton milestone. To those addressed in its first sentence, a quotation from St. Benedict's Rule for monks—"men who have no other purpose in life but God"—Merton swiftly asks, "is there any other purpose for anyone?" And though he insists that the book is only "a collection of personal notes on the Psalter," it is eminently theological at core. Being a poet as well as a contemplative he could place the psalms in their literary context as well as their theological one, with a delightful chapter on their poetry, symbolism, and typography. But he reaches his zenith in the chapter "Dark Lightning" in which he swings all meanings into a contemplative orbit, where one ascends into their silence and enters into their mystery by love.

Before leaving for the Orient, Thomas Merton compiled a chronological list of his published works, noting each category. There were five listed as "theology," nine as "religion." Of the former are the following: *The Ascent to Truth* (1951), an introduction to the doctrine of St. John of the Cross; *Bread in the Wilderness* (1953), of which we have just spoken; *The Last of the Fathers* (1954), a new translation of the encyclical commemorating the eighth centenary of the death of St. Bernard, *Doctor Mellifluous*, together with an erudite commentary, and two introductory chapters on St. Bernard and his writings; *The Living Bread* (1956), a book on the Eucharist; and *The New Man* (1961), a meditative volume, theologically textured, whose central theme is the question of "spiritual identity." Of the latter category, "religion," are: *Seeds of Contemplation* (1949), commented on above; *No Man Is an Island* (1955), personal reflections and meditations on the basic verities on which the spiritual life depends—a practical book for Everyman; *The Silent Life* (1957), a book on monasticism, and monks: cenobite (Benedictines and Cistercians) and eremite (Carthusians and Camaldolese); *Spiritual Direction and Meditation* (1960), a revised and somewhat expanded version of articles which first appeared in *Sponsa Regis; The Wisdom of the Desert* (1960), a selection, translation, and arrangement of 150 sayings of the Desert Fathers, from Migne's *Latin Patrology*, Vol. 73, with an introduction presenting these hermits (for the most part of Nitria and Scete), as "ahead of their time"; *New Seeds of Contemplation* (1961), published twelve years after the first, which Merton called an almost completely new book. Whereas the first—marvel as it was—recounted in a sort of isolation his own contemplative experience, the years between taught him to confront the needs and problems of other men, his solitude having met other solitudes ". . . with the loneliness, the simplicity, the perplexity of novices and scholastics of his monastic community: with the loneliness of people outside any monastery! with the loneliness of people outside the Church . . ." (*New Seeds of Contemplation*, p. ix). In this immensely broadened perspective even the word

contemplation receives a different emphasis, for he now sees
it in sharper theological focus, has *lived* it longer, and *seen it
lived* in others. If in the first version he might have appeared
to be trying to teach the reader how to become a contemplative, he was not. "One might as well write a book: How to
be an angel," he comments, and adds new descriptive notes
on the contemplative experience which "the reader will pe-
ruse at his own risk." Because of the varied kinds of spirituality some will not need a book like this; to some it will
have no meaning; but, "There are perhaps people without
formal religious affiliations who will find in these pages something that appeals to them. If they do, I am glad, as I feel
myself a debtor more to them than to the others." *Life and
Holiness* (1963) emphasizes basic ideas in the spiritual life
and the "one way" that leads to God, with a "theology of
work" set in a context that precludes any distinction between
the holiness of the layman and that of the religious, since
each Christian participates in the *active* life; *Seasons of Celebration* (1965) is a selection of essays and addresses dealing
with the four seasons of liturgical celebration, most of which
have been presented to, and in some cases discussed with,
specific groups or a congregation; they lead an *open* discussion on topics ranging from "Liturgy and Spiritual Personalism," to "Liturgical Renewal: Open Approach."

Beyond the above books distinctly labeled as "theology,"
and "religion," there are the numerous book reviews, prefaces, and introductions to the books of others, essays,
addresses, even broadsides, whether dealing specifically with
spiritual subjects or sociological themes—race, or the problems
of war—all of deep concern to him, and preeminently his
poems, all of which are vibrant with the spirit of this "new
man" of a spiritual genius rare in any century. All he has
written is situated in the Christian context of justice and
charity with the unction of a spirit reaching out to all people,
especially to the poor and the suffering.

Some of his latest writings deal with primitives, the simplicity of whose cults and cultures had fascinated him for a
long time, such as the Zapotecan culture of the Oaxaca Val-

ley, Monte Alban and classic Mayan, and post-classic Mexican (Toltec and Aztec) in the five centuries preceding the Spanish conquest—simple peoples who were conscious not so much of *traveling* toward some future goal, but *having arrived*, of being at the very heart of things. And I recall marvelous lines which he had written the day of my last visit and read to me from his (then in progress) long work "The Geography of Lograire."

There is also his writing (spiritual writing surely) that grew out of his involvement in *aggiornamento*, such as notes, addresses, proposals, and reports that, though circulated among Trappist-Cistercian monasteries, have never reached the public. Merton saw monastic renewal as a renewal of the *wholeness* of monastic life in its charismatic authenticity, and though focus be set on the traditional ideal, it must be tempered by a certain realism and common sense. At the second American meeting of Cistercian abbots of North and South America, held at Gethsemani, October, 1964, in his official capacity of Novice Master, he could give his suggestions for adaptation of the monastic life, specifics for the formation of young monks, and also—a theme close to his heart—a renewal of eremetism within it. He suggested that the abbots seriously consider the creation of a "hermitage" or *laura* to be attached to one of the monasteries in North America, in which those who felt called to the solitary life might try out their call. Gethsemani was one of the monasteries he suggested, another Snowmass, and he offered to help with the experiment. How providentially this worked out for him is well known. A cinder-block cabin hidden on a wooded hill about a mile from the monastery had, at his suggestion, been built some time previous for purposes of ecumenical dialogue with leaders of various faiths who came to visit him. He had already been permitted to spend some of his free time there. Already in 1955 he had had hopes of someday becoming a quasi-hermit, when he was put in full charge of the forest, with a fire-lookout-post on their highest hill. But in the summer of 1965, the time came close when he would take over the hermitage permanently: "I am semi-permanent there already. It is wonderful to live so close to the birds, etc. I want to get the wood around there made into a game sanctuary . . ." (letter, June 16, 1965). But on August 17 the happy news came, "This week I officially begin the hermit life. . . . Thereafter I was given careful accounts of the fauna and flora surrounding the cabin, deer, chipmunks, foxes, quail, and birds of every description; his rose-hedge, daffodils, crocus, and day-lilies. Somewhat later he said, "I am now pushing fifty and realize more and more that every day is just a free gift. . . . The 'I' that goes from day to day is not an important 'I' and his future matters little. And the deeper 'I' is in an eternal present. If a door should one day open from one realm to the other, then 'I' (whoever that is!) will be glad of it" (letter, September 17, 1965).

There are few things that Thomas Merton spoke of more constantly and consistently than solitude. In *Disputed Questions* there is a chapter titled "A Philosophy of Solitude," of which he said, "That's what I really have to say!" In 1955 he had sent me an offprint of an article that had appeared in *Témoignages*, in March, a publication of La Pierre-Qui-Vire, a Benedictine Abbey in France. On its olive-green paper cover he had written, "This is rare, controversial, has not appeared in English, only in French and Italian—and is very personal." Throughout his writings one is conscious of the spiritual ambience of the solitude he tasted at his hermitage, notably in "Day of a Stranger" (which I consider one of the peaks of his writing) done for a South American editor to describe a "typical day" in his life, sometime in May, 1965. This essay, rewritten and slightly amplified, appeared in *The Hudson Review*. Another essay on the solitary life, "Love and Solitude," originally written as a preface for the Japanese translation of *Thoughts in Solitude*, was revised to form an essay on "the solitary life, on contemplation, and on basic monastic values which are today called into question even by the monks themselves." Not that he would elaborate a "defense" of solitude, but in his words, "let solitude speak a little and say something for itself." The corrections, deletions, and insertions on these nine pages of manuscript show with what concern and care he had labored over it. An article on "Christian Solitude," subtitled "Notes on an Experiment," having to do with the hermit life at Gethsemani, according to my manuscript, was published at Harvard. Suffice these instances to show that in Merton's opinion solitude and the silence which it entailed were the *sine qua non* of any life of the spirit and those who wish to become solitary are, as a rule, solitary already: "At most they are not aware of their condition. In which case all they need is to discover it. But in reality, all men are solitary. Only most of them are so averse to being alone, or to feeling alone that they do everything they can to forget their solitude" (*Disputed Questions*, p. 178). They do this he says, by what Pascal called "divertissement" (diversion, systematic distraction) "so mercifully provided by society, which enables a man to avoid his own company for twenty-four hours a day." This treatise, "A Philosophy of Solitude," is one of the finest to be found anywhere today. Another, "Love and Need: Is Love a Package or a Message?" (September, 1966), which as far as I know is still in manuscript, is another of like kin. For our entire attitude toward life will be "in one way or another an attitude toward love."

Thomas Merton's vital interest in Eastern thought and monasticism, in which in recent years he became something of an expert and was so considered by monks of Buddhist as well as of Christian tradition, is a tremendously significant facet of his writing career. It was this interest that led to his journey to Asia and death in Bangkok. The point was poignantly made by Abbot Flavian, when in his homily to his monks referred to earlier, he told of their having talked of death before he left "first jokingly, then seriously. He was ready for it. He even saw a certain fittingness in dying over there amidst those Asian monks, who symbolized for him man's ancient and perennial desire for the deep things of God."

This interest of Merton's had an early beginning. In one of the most engaging passages in *The Seven Storey Mountain*, he tells of his meeting with the Hindu monk Bramachari, of whom he became very fond, and credits him with suggesting Augustine's *Confessions* for his reading, and the *Following of Christ*, a new departure for Thomas Merton as "it is rather ironical that I had turned spontaneously to the East, in reading about mysticism, as if there were little or nothing in the Christian tradition." At that time too he was reviewing Aldous Huxley's *Ends and Means*, in which he found him quoting John of the Cross and Theresa of Avila, and "less orthodox writers like Meister Eckhart," who became one of Merton's favorites. But his spiritual tastes ran preferentially to the Orient. He tells of "ransacking the university library for books on Oriental mysticism," beginning his reading with Wieger's French translation of hundreds of strange Oriental texts, distantly prophetic of his own later gathering of texts of the Desert Fathers and, more importantly, his translation of texts and poems, which resulted from a meditative reading in Chuang Tzŭ, whom he called the most spiritual of the Chinese philosophers, and the chief authentic historical spokesman for Taoism. In a graph he once made of what he considered his best books, *The Way of Chuang Tzŭ* rated highest, and was the one he most enjoyed doing. I would judge that by far the bulk of his *spiritual* writings in the last years was on some facet of Eastern mysticism, with a good beginning in his dialogue with D. T. Suzuki, in 1961. Already in the late fifties he had begun not only to review books dealing with Zen mysticism, since he felt "that we can filter a little Zen into our lives without losing our soul or becoming beatniks," but prefaces and introductions for them as well. In 1960 he translated the *Ox Mountain Parable* of Meng Tzu, based on a literal translation under Chinese ideograms; *Jubilee*, January, 1961, published an article on "Classic Chinese Thought"; in 1963 a book review of *The Platform Scripture*, an Asian Institute translation by Wing-Tsit Chan, a manuscript which forms part of the appendix to the first chapter of Merton's *Mystics and Zen Masters*. One could go on and on. . . .

In that marvelous journal of personal notes, meditations,

and opinions, *Conjectures of a Guilty Bystander*, he speaks of
the tone and temper of his interior world naming it

> . . . a Christian resonance which will sound in me as long
> as I am on earth, and perhaps in heaven, and in the new
> creation, in the world to come. It is the tone of fourteenth-
> century mysticism, of the Latin Fathers, of twelfth-century
> monasticism, but it is open also to China, to Confucianism
> and to Zen, to the great Taoists. All this is not purely su-
> pernatural, doubtless: and yet it is precisely in this quasi-
> sacramental way, by means of this cultural matter with a
> mysterious Christian form, that God works in our lives,
> since we are creatures of history, and tradition is vitally im-
> portant to us. (*Conjectures of a Guilty Bystander*, p. 167)

He delighted in his visitors from the East, and over a number
of years carried on a rich dialogue with certain writers and
notable representatives of Eastern monasticism: his friend,
John C. H. Wu, to whose *Golden Age of Zen* he wrote an
introduction, and the Vietnamese monk, Thich Nhat Hanh,
to name but two. In a letter of June 7, 1966, he wrote: "Incidentally, the Buddhist from Vietnam, Thich Nhat Hanh was
here—a fine guy altogether. I liked him very much. We made
a tape together for Dan Berrigan in which we do everything
including sing, he a Buddhist Gatha, I a Cistercian Alleluia."

But the quintessence of Thomas Merton's thought on Zen
is gathered in the essays that comprise one of his last published books, *Zen and the Birds of Appetite* (1968), and especially in its enlightening first essay, "The Study of Zen,"
first published in *Cimarron Review*, Oklahoma State University, June, 1968. In a key passage he says that "we begin to
divine that Zen is not only beyond the formulations of Buddhism but it is also in a certain way 'beyond' (and even
pointed to by) the revealed message of Christianity. When
one breaks through the limits of cultural and structural
religion—or irreligion—one is liable to end up by a 'birth in
the spirit' or just by intellectual awakening, in a simple void
where all is liberty because all is actionless action" (*Zen and
the Birds of Appetite*, p. 8). This is the Chinese *Wuwei* that

so appealed to him and that he likens to the New Testament "freedom of the sons of God." Not that he held them to be theologically one and the same, but "they have at any rate the same kind of limitlessness, the same lack of inhibition, the same psychic fullness of creativity that mark the fully integrated maturity of the 'enlightened self'" (*ibid.*, p. 8).

At the core of man's binding to God Merton sensed a certain common element—this (in his trip to Asia) he would examine at first hand, and in this ecumenical age prepare himself for what might have been the cumulative peak of all his writing, an ecumenical interpretation of mysticism. For Thomas Merton was a man who believed that prayer, meditation, and contemplation had no place in the margins of life, even in our technological world, but at its very heart. It is a way of living, since man's deepest need is "the direct and pure experience of reality in its ultimate root. . . . contemplation must be possible if man is to remain human." Since the days of St. Bernard and the Golden Age of Cistercian mysticism there has not been a spokesman for contemplative life such as Thomas Merton. For men of all faiths he has been a pervasive influence in our century, and when lesser names have been forgotten the name of Thomas Merton will be remembered.

Not long ago, speaking of Merton's friends, Naomi Burton said to me, "Each of us knows a different Thomas Merton." I agreed. He was a man who had the happy gift of going out to each person in a unique way, that they might touch him at that particular depth of spirit that answered most their love and their need. He had well read his Aelred of Rievaulx with his "theology of friendship," and considered friendship with another human being as an epiphany of friendship with God, a new creation in Christ. I knew him perhaps most in his "inner self," as he shared with me many luminous moments (and moments not so luminous, as is the privilege of friendship with its inviolable silences). On the occasion of a display of his manuscripts and memorabilia at Mount St. Paul College, where I taught, he wrote a beautiful letter to the students in which he spoke of "an *absence* that is a *presence*." This it will always be for his friends—and every man *was* and *is* his friend. For Thomas Merton was a man for all men, who came into our contemporary world with no program— but the gift of himself.

CHARLES DUMONT

THE CONTEMPLATIVE

When I was asked to speak of Father Thomas Merton at this session,* a sentence by Cardinal Suhard came to my mind at once: "It is not by proportions in the abstract that we reconcile the two words which are often mistakenly set up as contrasts: action and contemplation, there is a living synthesis of them, which is holiness." It is not my intention to suggest Father Merton for canonization; with his horror of all formality, I think he would rather work a miracle if he were threatened with inscription in the catalogue of saints. But it seems to me that he achieved that living synthesis of which the Archbishop of Paris spoke, a synthesis always fragile, like life, always to be begun again, always to be rectified, but always more "comprehensive," in both senses of the word, until it grasps all, understands everything, to lead everything back to God. "All is yours, and you are Christ's."

A CONFLICTING PERSONALITY

Born in Provence, the child of a New Zealand artist father and an American mother who met in Paris and were married in London, Thomas Merton was a student at Cambridge, then at Columbia. He entered Gethsemani Abbey in Kentucky on December 10, 1941, and met his death accidentally at Bangkok on December 10, 1968.

Father Merton is too well known for me to say any more.

* An ecumenical session held at Ramegnies-Chin (Tournai) Belgium, in July, 1969. This article first appeared in French, "Recherche oecuménique: prière et action," Ed. C.D.D., Tournai; and an English translation later was published in *Lumen Vitae*, Vol. XXIV (1969), 4.—EDITOR.

He has also written his life, up to his first years as a monk, in *The Seven Storey Mountain* (or *Elected Silence* in England), a book which has had considerable success in America and all over the world. This success in print showed him how eager for the spiritual life his contemporaries outside the monastery were, and brought him into contact with the men of his time. But he remained a monk all his life and rarely left his abbey. A paradox which is not so uncommon in history, his seeking for greater solitude, went together with an ever-increasing literary activity, ever-greater involvement in the world. This did not happen without difficulties and exterior clashes, without interior conflicts. But a certain humor, that flower of wisdom, always made him recover his balance.

Exuberant by nature, he wanted to be more active and more contemplative than his rule and his abbot could allow. His abbot told me that Father Louis was the monk who had given him the most anxieties and problems, but added immediately that out of the four or five hundred monks he had known, no one had been more humble and more obedient. From a superior who had known him for nearly thirty years, this testimonial, given during his lifetime, is very considerable.

He was versatile, changeable even, and his successive and sometimes contradictory enthusiasms were confusing. Here is an example: "The temptation of monastic life is to evade this austere responsibility by falling back into passive indifference, thinly veiled resentment disguised as obedience and abandonment. Since in fact one *need not* positively accept what happens, one can be merely resigned and negative. . . . The worst temptation . . . is simply to give up asking and seeking. To leave everything to the superiors in this life and to God in the next . . ." (*Conjectures of a Guilty Bystander*, p. 166).

And yet he had written in this same journal ten pages earlier:

The basic sin, for Christianity, is rejecting others in order to choose oneself, deciding *against* others and deciding *for* oneself. Why is this sin so basic? Because the idea that you can choose yourself, approve yourself, and then offer yourself (fully "chosen" and "approved") to God, applies the assertion of yourself over against God. . . . In such a religion the Cross becomes meaningless except as the (blasphemous) certification that because you suffer, because you are misunderstood, you are justified twice over—you are a martyr. Martyr means witness. You are then a witness? To what? To your own infallible light and your own justice, which you have *chosen*. (*Conjectures*, p. 157)

This apparent conflict between personal responsibility and obedience pursued Father Merton all his life, and if he could not formulate a synthesis clearly, his actions achieved it. To fix one's own choice is to set up a screen to the influence of Christ. He confided to his Journal this confession of a Christian writer:

My acts are meaningful, not merely when I do what I consider right (still less when I do what I imagine will let me be at peace with myself) but when my acts accord with the goodness and blessedness which are in man and in the world by reason of Christ's love.

This is the great flaw in my writing and in my life. I, too, rarely act in the full awareness of what it means that I am a Christian. But, on the other hand, my fidelity to Christ demands that I avoid too facile a recourse to Christian unction and pious phrases. (*Conjectures*, pp. 244–45)

CRITICISM OF TRADITION

I would like to talk to you of Catholic tradition on the subject of "prayer and action" by putting before you one of its most recent representatives, Father Thomas Merton. Nourished on this tradition, in its most varied and purest expressions, ancient and medieval, he loved it and lived on it, but he criticized it, too, and wished to get beyond it, in order to make it more "relevant" as the modern English vocabulary would say:

A monasticism that simply affirms these religious and cultural values, even on the highest "spiritual level," has had its day. . . . it is in fact the monasticism I myself entered, to which I was called, for which my own past had in great measure prepared me. I still love it, but I see I must "renounce" it in the sense of transcending it—for in the face of death it is not yet quite enough. It will "do," of course: but at the risk of evasion from the realities of our present situation, and the abdication of present responsibilities to God's word in the world. (*Conjectures*, p. 162)

If he criticized this tradition, he realized that he was a link in its chain:

All this [medieval world] was in some way sacramental, and all of it had me turning somewhere, I did not know where.
   Now I live in a world which is to some extent (though at least I am in a monastery) bare of all such meanings and such signs. The place I am in does, nevertheless, have something of this climate. However, it is trying to lose the climate and substitute another. What other? I cannot say, I do not know. For my own part, I know I must keep alive in myself what I have once known and grown into: and if anyone else wants a part of it, I can try to pass it on. (*Conjectures*, p. 169)

There are sentences of this kind in *The City of God* by St. Augustine, who also lived toward the end of a culture. The Church is not bound up with a mortal civilization, but something of it is to be transmitted to the Christians of tomorrow.

As everyone does, Thomas Merton had studied the problem of the relations between contemplation and action. He did so all the more attentively from the fact that for him it was a personal problem. Like everyone, too, he had encountered the difficulties of a vocabulary which has become ambiguous, from signifying many different things in the course of the history of Greek and Christian thought. The most regrettable confusion arises from transposing into terms of states of life or of religious orders what was, for men like St. Augustine, St. Gregory the Great, or St. Bernard, the expression of an interior and psychological conflict. Recollection, the serenity of interior prayer, of reflection, of meditation, obviously suffer from the fatigue, the many cares, and at times the dispersion of mind, which are inevitably connected with dedication to the material or spiritual needs of men. It is chiefly from St. Thomas, we think, that this rigid classification into states of life imposes itself. St. Thomas applied the categories of Aristotle, for whom the contemplative cannot act at all without deviating, without losing control of his reasoning faculties. . . . From this soon grows that triumphalism of "contemplatives," the superiority of the contemplative orders, and this classification has found its place in the Canon Law of the western Church.

But these distinctions which are, no doubt, useful to group together those who hear more or less the same call, or who belong to one family of spirit, who are also looking for a fairly similar type of existence, these distinctions, when they are institutionalized in rigid fashion, attack the liberty of the Holy Spirit, and are in danger of imposing a kind of life which very quickly becomes conventional:

> The best is not the ideal. Where what is theoretically best is imposed on everyone as the *norm*, then there is no longer any room even to be good. The best, imposed as a norm, becomes evil.
> One might argue that the best, the highest, is imposed on all in monasteries. Far from it: St. Benedict's principle is that the Rule should be moderate, so that the strong may desire to do more and the weak may not be overwhelmed and driven out of the cloister.
> You must be free, and not involved. (*Ibid.,* pp. 82–83)

The doctrine of St. Bernard and the Cistercians of his school, notably Aelred of Rievaulx, is obviously anterior to the classification of the religious orders. Their teaching about prayer and action is very supple, very alive to the situations of life, to the dispositions of each one, and above all, to the human condition, which is not absolute; in a proportion which does not differ very much between individuals, we are all both contemplative and active.

Thomas Merton has studied St. Bernard's position toward

our subject, in a book entitled *Marthe, Marie et Lazare.**
The title itself declares that there is a trichotomy for St. Bernard—action, contemplation, penance—and that he cannot be
counted among those who keep to the traditional duality. Father Merton grasped this thoroughly, and we read in his
preface:

> What exactly does St. Bernard mean by active life and
> contemplative life? In our time when we look at everything
> from the outside, instead of understanding it from within,
> when we judge by appearances rather than by the heart, we
> imagine that to distinguish the contemplative from the ac-
> tive life, it is enough to underline the question of enclo-
> sure. The contemplative life is that which is lived behind a
> wall, a cloistered life; the active life is that which is lived
> outside the enclosure, in the market place. In our over-sim-
> ple view of things, the contemplative life is defined by the
> absence of active works. Contemplative orders then are
> those which do not preach, or teach, or work in a hospital.
> Yes, well what do they do? . . . We distinguish the active
> from the contemplative religious not by showing who they
> are, but simply by pointing out where they are: not by
> showing what they are, but simply pointing out what they
> do. (*Marthe, Marie et Lazare*, Desclée De Brouwer, 1956,
> pp. 12–13)

It is very well said, but after this very personal introduction, Merton's study is deceptive. He seems to remain a
prisoner himself of the accepted categories. He undertakes his
study with the obvious desire of proving the superiority of the
contemplative life, but St. Bernard on this point, is more surprising, more versatile even than Merton. He even says at
times that Martha or Lazarus lead a superior life, and that in
any case, apostolic action is superior to any other, since it
presupposes contemplation.

In other studies or articles, Father Merton has suggested
other solutions. For example, that in a community, some do
everything like active people, even prayer, while others do everything like contemplative people, even work; or else, that it

---

* This volume was published only in French.—EDITOR.

is the community, mystical body in miniature, which fulfills the three states, each one performing one of the vocations. This specialization is dangerous for the life of the community. In fact, the contemplative life, the life of prayer, is required from all, for it listens for the Word of God in *lectio*, prayer and meditation. Each one practices it according to his means and to the possibilities of a common life which has its spiritual and material necessities. It is usually in a certain alternation and balance that Cistercians have seen the ideal in this domain.

In any case, perfection is not a personal affair. We are the members of the Mystical Body of Christ, and the perfection of one member consists in being perfectly integrated into the whole body. Here, Father Merton has also studied the history of the doctrine of the apostolic role of contemplatives. Several times, he has quoted a phrase of St. Augustine in *Contra Faustum*, in which contemplation is called sterile if it has no complement of apostolic activity. He endeavors to trace the beginning of this doctrine and concludes: "Unless I am mistaken, St. Teresa and the mystics of the sixteenth century were the first to stress the apostolic role of purely contemplative religious and their usefulness in the Church" (*ibid.,* p. 90). When did this doctrine begin, which would only find its accurate expression with Pius XI and the Letter to the Carthusians *Umbratilem?* Dom Francois Vandenbroucke draws attention to it already in the influence of the Cistercians of the twelfth century, especially among the mystics of Flanders or the Rhineland in the thirteenth century: Lutgarde, Mechtilde or Gertrude, or again in St. Catherine of Siena. Father Merton does not perceive its existence before the sixteenth century, while Father Urs von Balthasar only sees its full elaboration with Therese of Lisieux. Let us note in passing that it seems to have been women who had the intuition of this mysterious influence of prayer. Such a mystical union of souls is also solidly founded on the dogma of the communion of saints. That doctrine will remain at the heart of Merton's activity and prayer during the last ten years of his life.

It forms the basis, and guarantees the efficacy of all prayer and, by the same token, of all activity in the world.

"Solitude has its own special work: a deepening of awareness that the world needs. A struggle against alienation. True solitude is deeply aware of the world's needs" (*Conjectures*, p. 10). He wrote again in the preface to the Japanese edition of *The Seven Storey Mountain* (1965): "My monastery is not a home. It is not a place where I am rooted and established on the earth. It is not an environment in which I become aware of myself as an individual, but rather a place in which I disappear from the world as an object of interest in order to be everywhere in it by hiddenness and compassion. To exist everywhere I have to be No-one."

The strange coincidence has been noted that his last recorded words in this world were those with which he concluded his conference at Bangkok: "And now I will disappear." He understood the meaning of what had been so hard for him, the renunciation of that false self, in the trial of common life. He was fond of the symbolism of Jonas, because before being a prophet, we must live as he did, in the obscurity of the belly of the whale.

The contempt for the world, *contemptus mundi*, so sharp, so disdainful in his early writings, in which the world was portrayed as evil itself, chaos, the disintegration of personality, this contempt turned into compassion for the world that is passing away. Compassion and comprehension—these words flow from his pen unceasingly during his last years. He who, at the outset of his monastic life, readily pitched his tent on the summit of Mount Thabor or Mount Carmel, at the end of his life often pictured himself in the ditch of the parable of the Good Samaritan. And his only advantage over his companion in misfortune, his brother in the world, is that he can call the Good Samaritan, Christ, when He passes that way.

ECUMENICAL CONCERN

He became interested very early in ecumenism and was a pioneer of ecumenical encounters in America. He had a very spiritual form of prayer for Christian unity: "If I can unite *in myself* the thought and the devotion of Eastern and Western Christendom, the Greek and the Latin Fathers, the Russians with the Spanish mystics, I can prepare in myself the reunion of divided Christians. From that secret and unspoken unity in myself can eventually come a visible and manifest unity of all Christians. . . . We must contain all divided worlds in ourselves and transcend them in Christ" (*Conjectures*, p. 12).

But ecumenism soon extended for him to non-Christians of the religions of the Far East, of Islam and even to unbelievers. Through his studies in Zen Buddhism and the Sufis, he became an interpreter of the Christian mystics for the Far East, and of the Oriental disciplines for Christians. He corresponded with many spiritual people of all religions, with poets and artists who were unbelievers but who came to see him. He began to perceive a new meaning to give to his life of prayer. He used to say that one of the most important, and one of the most unheeded, aspects of ecumenism was the very special contribution which men of prayer, monks and religious in the world could make toward dialogue and approach, not only between Christians, but also with the ancient non-Christian religions. The *simplex intuitus veritatis*, the immediate perception of truth, is not merely metaphysical, it is also the common ground of all serious religious experience.

Merton wrote of this in *Mystics and Zen Masters:*

> Needless to say, the "contemplative" in the context of the present study, is not simply a person who, by vocation, is juridically isolated and cloistered. The mere fact of breaking off communication with the world and of losing interest in it certainly does not make one *ipso facto* a "contemplative." On the contrary, it would seem that today a certain openness to the world and a genuine participation in its anguish would normally help to safeguard the sincerity of a commitment to contemplation. ("Contemplation and Dialogue," p. 203)

Thomas Merton wrote those lines in an article in 1965, which was entirely devoted to this encounter of contemplatives or mystics beyond the barriers of creed. After examining the difficulties and chances of such a project, he concluded by insisting on a better understanding of what true mysticism is, real Christian contemplation, too much cried down or neglected in our time, or placed too high with ecstasies and visions. Faith should normally develop into mysticism, and if we do not go as far as that, right to the end of our faith, we do not present the whole truth which men expect from us, especially those whom a natural religious disposition has prepared to receive it in its fullness. Mysticism is a view of profound and penetrating faith into the mysteries of the kenosis, the Cross, the Resurrection, the pleroma, and the love of Christ which surpasses all knowledge.

Writing on "The Contemplative and the Atheist" (later published in *Contemplation in a World of Action*) Merton pointed out again:

> in all contemplative traditions, it has been found necessary that those who have attained to some depth of religious insight should to some extent guide others who seek to attain the same experience of truth in their own lives. Thus, though the contemplative lives in silence and seeks to maintain a certain freedom from involvement in feverish and pointless activity, he does not simply turn his back on the world of other men. Like them he remains rooted in this world. He remains open to the world and is ready, when necessary, to share with others something of his own experience, to the extent that this may be desirable or possible. He also realizes his need to listen to other men and learn from them.

OPENNESS TO THE WORLD

Since the Council particularly, the Catholic Church has entered into dialogue with modern man, with non-Christian religions, with atheists. The question, therefore, arises for the monk: should he too come into contact with this modern world, with non-Christian monks, with atheists? The question is not a simple one. Obviously, his first duty is to live his life of prayer, in solitude and silence, of listening for the

Word of God. And in doing this he serves the Church, as it was said at the Council: "Tradition . . . develops in the Church with the help of the Holy Spirit. For there is a growth in the understanding of the realities and the words which have been handed down. This happens through the contemplation and study made by believers, who treasure these things in their hearts, through the intimate understanding of spiritual things they experience. . . . For as the centuries succeed one another, the Church constantly moves forward towards the fulness of divine truth" (Vatican II, *Dogmatic Constitution on Divine Revelation*, ch. II, §. 8).

This silent and hidden life has no meaning unless it encourages attentive listening to God's Word, and makes it bear fruit. The depth of his vocation is a mystery for the monk which partially escapes him. In *Seasons of Celebration* Father Merton expressed this extremely well:

Formed by the discipline of a hidden wisdom, monks become themselves as hidden as wisdom is herself. They remain in this mortal life, and yet their life is already hidden with Christ in God and their citizenship is in heaven. They do not expect to be understood by men because they do not fully understand themselves. They realize that their silence is something of a problem and a scandal to those who happen to notice it: but they cannot fully explain the mystery to anyone. They are, themselves, too much a part of the mystery of silence to be able to formulate an apologetic for their own lives. Like wisdom, they manifest themselves by remaining hidden. That is why it is very important to remember that the monk, the solitary, cannot clearly explain himself to the rest of the world, and he is very foolish if he attempts to do so. What a tragedy for a monk to expound what he conceives to be a clear, definite, easily understandable explanation for his monastic life, for his vocation to be hidden in God! That means he has made the mistake of convincing himself that he understands the mystery of his vocation. Does he really understand? Then there is no more mystery! And if there is no more mystery, are we not perhaps forced to say there is no longer any vocation? (pp. 211–12)

Father Merton never departed from this very clear conviction about a monk's life. But he also believed more and more that monasteries today really had the duty of being centers where many Christians, young people especially, could find an answer to their spiritual aspirations, an answer they would otherwise go and seek elsewhere than in the Church.

He himself practiced this openness in the measure that was permitted him. He had a charism for it, and he easily forgot this when he imagined that he would find many prophets of his own capacity in all monasteries. This charism is grafted on to natural gifts. Isaias was a poet, and so was Merton, but prophets and poets are rare.

It even seemed to him that this openness, this existential dialogue with men and women of all vocations, would lead the monk to a better awareness of his own vocation.

THE DIFFICULT PATHS

But the paths of this openness of cloister are difficult. To open the doors of the cloister without discrimination is to disturb without hope of remedy that solitude and silence which are exactly what the world comes to find in monasteries. In Merton's case, it would have meant becoming the victim of publicity. Nevertheless, if his superiors were right in preserving him from it, sometimes in spite of him, the principle which they invoked seemed to him excessive. In a letter to me he wrote:

I do not think that it is valid and Christian to adopt a set of principles that one will renounce all apostolic activity regardless of circumstances, because this in effect is telling God you know His business better than He does. It is normal when one matures in the monastic life for certain contacts to become an obligation of charity. To simply say: "Because I am a monk I am absolutely bound to enclosure and must never go to any ecumenical dialogues, must never attend any conferences," is simply an evasion of God's Will. The true attitude, it seems to me, is to adopt a strict policy of separation from the world which nevertheless can admit of obvious exceptions, and then pursue the course of judging by *discretio spirituum*. (Letter, October 18, 1965.)

The exterior difficulties of such an activity of communication are not the most important ones. Exchange and sharing of spiritual experiences require prudence and great circumspection. Father Merton said this in some very fine pages in *Seeds of Contemplation*, the book, which, as he said, almost writes itself in a monastery. The chapter is called "Contemplata aliis tradere," and we quote a few passages from it:

If we experience God in contemplation, we experience Him not for ourselves alone but also for others. Yet if your experience of God comes from God, one of the signs may be a great diffidence in telling others about it. . . . No one is more shy than a contemplative about his contemplation. Sometimes it gives him almost physical pain to speak to anyone of what he has seen of God. Or at least, it is intolerable for him to speak about it as his own experience. At the same time, he most earnestly wants everybody else to share his peace and his joy. His contemplation gives him a new outlook on the world of men. He looks about him with a secret and tranquil surmise which he perhaps admits to no one, hoping to find in the faces of other men or to hear in their voices some sign of vocation and potentiality for the same deep happiness . . . or if he cannot speak to them, he writes for them, and his contemplative life is still imperfect without sharing, without companionship, without communion.

But the danger of being mistaken, the danger of speaking about what one has not experienced, remains great:

No one teaches contemplation except God Who gives it. The best you can do is to write something or say something that will serve as an occasion for some one else to realize what God wants of him. One of the worst things about an ill-timed effort to share the knowledge of contemplation with other people is that you assume that everybody else will want to see things from your own point of view when, as a matter of fact, they will not. They will raise objections . . . and you will find yourself in a theological controversy . . . and nothing is more useless for a contemplative than controversy. (*Seeds of Contemplation*, p. 189)

Merton continues in the same context:

Often we will do much more to make men contemplatives by leaving them alone and minding our own business . . . for our prayer and the grace that is given to us tend of their very nature to overflow invisibly through the Mystical Body of Christ, and we who dwell together invisibly in the bond of the One Spirit of God affect one another more than we can ever realize. . . . One who has a very little of this prayer . . . can do immense things for the souls of other men . . . but if he did try to start talking about it and reasoning about it, he would at once lose the little that he had of it.

But when God wishes to use us, He will make us do His work, even without our knowing it, and we will remain free from all vanity and calculation of our success, for "in actual practice, one of the last barricades of egoism, and one which many saints have refused to give up entirely, is this insistence on doing the work and getting the results and enjoying them ourselves." It remains that contemplation, like every good thing, demands to be shared, and each one only fully delights in it when it is possessed by all in common, but this perfection belongs to heaven alone.

A LIVING SYNTHESIS

The grouping of the elect is beginning; we can grasp something of it and rejoice over it. I would like to conclude by recalling a theme which was dear to Thomas Merton as a poet: the reconciliation, the union of all that he knew and loved, of all those with whom he felt linked by friendship, in time and in space. This grouping was at work within him and he liked to compare it to a symphony, to which he himself gave a meaning while listening to it. It is the mysterious symphony of souls at prayer. This image was also dear to St. Bernard who said "that nothing on earth resembled heaven so

closely as a choir singing the praises of God." It was likewise
an idea dear to Newman for whom, in the liturgy, each one
practices his part in the choir of the angels.

It was, however, in Clement of Alexandria that Merton
had found this musical idea wonderfully expressed. If the austere St. John of the Cross had been the first guide of the novice in his "ascent towards the light," it seems to me that
Clement was the favorite friend of his last years. In him he
recognized himself, and it is himself that he describes in his
introduction to some passages chosen from the *Protreptikos*
(*Clement of Alexandria: Selections from the Protreptikos*,
pp. 6–7):

> His manner is familiar and informal, his style is full of
> charm. His is an agile and witty mind, quick to reach out
> for images. . . . One feels that he is teaching the deepest
> truths with an ease and an assurance born of the convic-
> tion that Christ Himself was present in the gathering of
> disciples, Christ Himself was there imparting a teaching
> deeper than words. It was for this reason that speech and
> thought did not need to be strained to the utmost. What
> mattered most was the familiar *rapport* between teacher
> and disciple, and the Holy Spirit would do the rest.

The openness of the *Protreptikos* had enchanted Thomas
Merton, especially that passage in which Clement sees Christ
as God's great cantor, "He has structured the whole universe
musically, and the discord of elements He has brought together in an ordered symphony." Elsewhere he wrote ("In
Silentio" later published in *Seasons of Celebration*, p. 215)
"Now each man's individual song, that he sings in secret
with the Spirit of God, blends also in secret with the unheard
notes of every other individual song . . . these voices all form
a great choir whose music is heard only in the depths of silence, because it is more silent than the silence itself." In
Conjectures the same image reappears: "Our singing together
is perhaps the best and most evident manifestation of God in
His world: by His music in us. This is a deep reason for monastic psalmody: this, and the morning that our music is,
after all, out of tune" (p. 170).

If the great grace of the Council has been to make us more vividly aware of the universality of the Church in an ever more unified world, Thomas Merton, because he himself was unified in his inmost soul, because he was a poet also, knew how to perceive, to rediscover something of this harmony which exists between men and God, reconciled in Christ. He also knew how to communicate to many men and women a little of his own prayer and of his interior life, because in the desert of the cloister as in the desert of big cities, there is the same thirst for the living God, the same hunger for truth.

JAMES FOX

THE SPIRITUAL SON*

It was Tuesday, December 10, 1968, about fifteen minutes
before 1:00 in the afternoon. I was about to prepare a little
midday lunch, when I glanced out of one of the windows,
and saw the jeep from the Monastery pull up in the yard and
stop. No one ever comes at that hour, because the monks are
all at dinner in the Abbey. So I watched with curiosity to see
who might climb out of the jeep.

First came Brother Patrick. He had been my secretary for
some ten years while I was Abbot before he went to help out
at our General's House in Rome. On his return from Rome,
he was appointed secretary to Father Louis. The other person
who stepped out was Brother Lawrence, secretary to the new
Abbot.

I thought to myself: "What on earth is bringing these two
secretaries up here to the hermitage at this time when they
should be eating their dinner?" I anxiously opened the door
of the porch and they came in.

First, we made a little visit to Our Lord in our chapel.
Then all three of us came into the "study." Brother Patrick
spoke first. He said to me: "Reverend Father, you had better
sit down before I deliver the message which I have for you."

---

* While Abbot James Fox was superior at Gethsemani and after
his resignation, it was his custom to write "diaspora" letters to various monks of Gethsemani who were away from the monastery,
such as at our House of Studies in Rome, the foundations in Chile
or Oxford, North Carolina, as well as to monks on loan in our Hong
Kong monastery, etc. This letter was written several weeks after
Fr. Merton's death and circulated in mimeographed form. It was
revised and expanded in 1973 for publication here.—EDITOR.

I said: "Go ahead—shoot. I don't need to sit down for anything."

"Well, I think you better sit down."

I realized that this day, December 10, was my birthday, and probably they were up to some trick or other to help me celebrate. Perhaps Abbot Flavian had sent them up with a surprise dinner. I was determined they wouldn't pull any tricks on me.

Brother Patrick then said: "Well, O.K.—the message is that—that Father Louis is dead."

"You don't think I am going to swallow that, do you? What is really on your mind? Come on, tell me. What are you two really up to?"

"Really, the Abbot received a message from the State Department in Washington, D.C.," they said. Later a phone call came all the way from the American Embassy in Bangkok that Fr. Louis had been electrocuted by a faulty wire from a large electric fan in his room.

As it turned out, according to reports we received later, Fr. Louis had been in his wet bare feet, standing on the terrazzo floor. The electricity went right through him. Several hours later he was discovered lying on the floor with the electricity still flowing through him.

It seems that his death had been instantaneous—the instant that he had caught hold of that faulty wire. A large segment of his bare chest had been burned deeply, where the fan had fallen on him, pinning him down.

Br. Patrick continued: "Father Flavian sent us up to tell you the tragic news. We are to bring you back to the Abbey. Fr. Flavian wants to talk to you."

I looked at both Br. Patrick and Br. Lawrence in utter bewilderment. I saw only too clearly that indeed they were not joking. They were in deep sorrowful sincerity. Then I really sat down repeating over and over: "What a loss—what a loss."

Then I realized a strange coincidence—rather personal indeed. It was on December 10, 1941, my birthday, that Fr. Louis entered Gethsemani. And now, it was December 10,

1968, again, when he entered Eternity—his Birthday in Heaven—"Natalitia."

For some twenty-six years we had been intimate friends, in the mysterious arrangement of Divine Providence. How quickly those years had passed. My first meeting with Fr. Louis was as follows:

In July of 1942, he had been a novice for some eight months. At that time I was Retreat Master for guests who might come to the monastery to make a retreat. The summer of that year brought Fr. Louis' only brother, John Paul, for a visit. At that time, he was an officer in the Canadian Air Force, and was about to be sent overseas.

He came to Gethsemani for two reasons—one was, understandably, to visit his brother Tom—Fr. Louis—and to say "Au revoir." The other reason was that, following in the steps of his older brother, he was to be received into the Church. It was my duty to prepare him for Baptism, and for his First Communion.

During one of my first conferences with John Paul, to my astonishment, in bounced one of the novices. I could easily see that he was bursting with fervor and enthusiasm. I did not know him personally, but I asked him to wait outside for a while, until I finished my conference with John Paul.

The novice did this most graciously. However, his most expressive eyes pleaded with me, saying, "Please don't be too long. He's my brother—he's leaving soon for the War—I may never see him again." And so it was.

Since Fr. Louis was a novice, I had very little to do with him, because I was on the professed side of the house. In 1944, during the Feast of St. Benedict, I went with the pioneers to establish Gethsemani's first foundation, which was to be Our Lady of the Holy Spirit, near Conyers, Georgia.

Four years later, Divine Providence brought me back to Gethsemani to be superior. Thus, I was Fr. Louis' Abbot for the next twenty years. In turn, he was my Confessor for about the last fifteen of those years. Understandably, we were on more than ordinary intimate terms.

If the following points of information, chosen out of many

possible ones, contribute to a greater esteem of dear Fr. Louis
—not just as an author of prose or poetry, nor even as a gifted
director of others in the spiritual life, but one who himself
had persevered in striving for monastic perfection to the very
end of his life—then the purpose of this little resume will
have been achieved.

Furthermore, I not only deplore, but kindly ask your for-
giveness for all and every reference to myself in these pages. I
would certainly have omitted them if it were possible.
Though how else could I have told you about my relationship
to Fr. Louis? So be it.

One quality that endeared Fr. Louis to all the brethren
was his terrific "sense of humor." His sharp and penetrating
intellect enabled him to perceive the amusing and the comic,
seconds before almost anyone else. I noticed this, in Chapter
talks. "Chapter" is the time, whether in the evening before
Compline, or Sunday mornings after Lauds, when the entire
monastic family gathers in a large room outside the Church
proper. Usually at that time, the Abbot gives some spiritual
conference, and makes any announcements pertinent to the
family—such as, for example, new appointments or changes in
schedule, etc.

The monks all had seats around the wall, usually in rank of
seniority. The monk who sat on one side of Fr. Louis was Fr.
Paphnutius. He and Fr. Louis often had jousts of chivalrous,
humorous wit—each trying to "outsmart" the other.

One Sunday, Fr. Paphnutius changed his name—who could
blame him? It was my duty to announce the change to the
Community, so I said: "Our Fr. Paphnutius has received permission to change his name."

I looked down the line of monks on my right to Fr. Paphnutius. Of course I also saw Fr. Louis. The minute I mentioned Fr. Paphnutius, Fr. Louis was all alert, perhaps wondering to himself, "What's my sparring partner up to now?"

So I continued, in as serious a judicial voice as I could
muster, "Henceforth, he will be known in history as . . ." I
could see out of the corner of my eye that Fr. Louis was on
the edge of his seat. Then I stopped for a few seconds—for

effect—and, trying to sound like an astronaut concluding a message to Houston control, barked out: "ROGER!"

With that, Fr. Louis burst into laughter, clapped his hands on his knees, and almost rolled off onto the floor. Fr. Louis' laughter was ebullient—bubbling over. He looked at his neighbor, the erstwhile Paphnutius. Paphnutius, smiling wryly, looked back at Fr. Louis as if to say: "I put one over on you that time."

One time Fr. Louis had to go to the hospital for a minor operation. Since there were hardly any vacant rooms on the adult side of the hospital, Fr. Louis had to be content with a room in the Maternity Ward.

He wrote back to the Community: "Surrounded as I am by innocent tots, who continually praise the Lord, to adapt a quote from the Feast of the Holy Innocents, 'non loquendo, sed ululando. .'—'not by speaking but by yelling at the top of their voices'—I, cast out from the Paradise of the Gethsemani monks, and relegated to the Limbo of the Bardstown Mothers, I had almost lost my identity. Your reassuring letters, poems, etchings, etc., have managed to preserve my distracted wits, and I am once again convinced that I am still a member of our utterly unique monastic Community . . ."

Fr. Louis was very sensitive regarding the esteem and affection of his monastic brothers. I remember speaking to him about the hermit life, on which I myself was soon to embark. "You are an experienced hermit by now," I said. "What advice have you to give me?"

He said: "One thing that can cause you great suffering is this: You will be out there in solitude and seclusion. The thought will come to you that the Community has disowned you—scorns you—ostracized you, for good. This thought can torture you at times in a very excruciating manner."

A few weeks after that conversation, I put the same question to him. He gave me the same answer. Thus I concluded how keenly he desired the love of his brothers.

Another time he was in the hospital for several weeks. He returned home, and the next day came in to see me. "Reverend Father, give me a good penance," he said.

"What's up now?" I asked.

"Well, it's this way. I had often asked the Cellarer for several items. He seemed to ignore my requests. I had hard thoughts about him. Lo and behold, in my absence they have built a perfect private room for me, far better than I deserve —right next to the Novitiate Dormitory. Perfect for silence. When I returned yesterday, and saw the excellent job they had done after all my uncharitable thoughts and rash judgments—that room, that concrete expression of love and affection for me—I just sat on the edge of my bed and cried."

The custom used to be in our Order that in preparation for Ordination to the Priesthood a monk had to perform various public acts of "Penance." The idea was that one should make "reparation" for any possible disedification he may have been guilty of—or not guilty of. One of these "customs" was that the one to be ordained would "kiss the feet" of each member of the Community during the course of dinner.

In our Community, the tables are placed around the walls of the Refectory. At this side only do the monks sit, which leaves the sides of the tables facing the center of the room free and unobstructed, thus facilitating the serving of the monks.

The monks sit with their backs toward the walls and their feet toward the center. The monk performing this "Penance" gets down on his knees before each monk. The others stretch out their feet, covered with their robes—sometimes not too completely. The monk on his knees then grabs the outstretched shoe and kisses it.

Considering that sometimes we had about 250 to 270 monks in the Refectory, this was indeed a real "workout." The monk to be ordained usually took on only half the Community on the first day and the second half on the next day.

In the "good old days," a monk to be ordained also had to "beg his dinner." This consisted in going before each monk, at dinner time, on his knees, with a large bowl. He would hold the bowl up towards the monk at the table. The brother monk would then take a large spoonful of his own potatoes, cabbage, lima beans, etc.—whatever happened to be the "portion" for that day—and pour it into the "begging monk's" outstretched bowl. Sometimes a kind-hearted monk would put in a spoonful of his apple sauce, or cookies, or whatever the dessert for the day happened to be. When the begging monk's bowl was filled, he went back to his place to enjoy the fruits of his begging and the charity of his brothers.

When it came time for Fr. Louis to perform these "Penances," he was full of smiles and joy and happiness in his humbling sacrifices. Concerning him, as I watched the renowned author of *The Seven Storey Mountain* begging, on his two knees, before each of his brother monks, I could not help remarking inwardly: "How powerful is the Grace of Jesus—how lavish with Grace has Jesus been to Fr. Louis."

One may say that exterior acts of humility reveal a deep interior humility. But the sure test of genuine virtue, as St. Benedict says, is "Humility expressed through Obedience."

Fr. Louis had a highly emotional, "ex abrupto," and superdynamic nature. Yet he "worked at it" daily, and mastered it completely; that is to say, he brought himself successfully under the controlling influence of Jesus, if not at the first instant of struggle—"primo-primi" as one terms it—eventually. Only Jesus knows the heroic efforts he had to make at times. But it is in this very area of self-immolation and self-purgation, and not in his writings, that his true "greatness" really lies.

To relate one relatively small incident: Every year or every second year, one of the Higher Superiors would come from Europe for the Regular Visitation of our Community to make sure we were keeping to the true spirit of our vocation and to give wise counsel where needed. Since Fr. Louis was well-versed in so many foreign languages, he often served as an interpreter. Thus he would be on more than ordinary friendly terms with the Visitor.

As you know, at Gethsemani we have some fifty acres enclosed around the main buildings by a wall—not so much to keep the monks in, as to keep wandering "outsiders" out. Beyond the walls are our farms, fields and forests. The woods themselves stretch out for many hundreds of acres—ideal for silent communing with the "God of Nature." Our Father St. Bernard used to say: "I learn as much or more from running brooks than from written books."

Fr. Louis was an intense lover of these forests. His wandering through the sylvan valleys or "hollers," as they are called in the local "patois," provided him with a "balance" for his monastic day. Personally, I never found any objection to this truly monastic atmosphere which the deep woods provided.

However, during one Visitation a rather "legalistic-minded" monk complained to the Visitor that monks were "going outside the enclosure for walks." At the end of the Visitation, the Visitor would come to the Abbot with his "list" of points to be "improved on." Since Fr. Louis was the interpreter, I had him present to make sure I would get all "the points" correctly.

The Visitor mentioned several "points." Then he came to the "crucial" one, saying, "We are cloistered monks. Therefore we should not go out to the woods, outside the enclosure."

To me the point made little or no difference personally, since I had hardly time to myself with some 270 monks to look after. But I did know how keenly attached to these woodland walks Fr. Louis was. My heart leaped within; I looked at Fr. Louis. His face flushed red and big tears filled his eyes. He quivered a bit, but never said a word. He remained silent, seemingly crushed. To think that that one "exercise" which he loved so much, and legitimately, was to be denied him! Many thoughts ran through my mind, but I concluded that there was no need arguing then.

I began to ponder about those woods. In Europe, most of our monasteries, since the French Revolution and other wars, have very little acreage. They are surrounded by families. Their wooded lands outside their enclosure walls are practically in the public domain. Monks can hardly go out in their woodlands without meeting with secular people.

Our situation is entirely different. Our acreage is so large that families are miles away from us. More important, the monks go to our woods during the manual work period to cut down excessive growth of trees and prepare firewood for heating the Abbey in the winter. It is a regular and recognized part of our monastic life.

We did need someone to supervise our forests so that they be kept well cleared of fallen trees, and so that the right trees be marked for firewood and others for timber with which to do carpentry work like building sheds, etc. Who would be more skilled and knowledgeable as our "Chief Ranger of the Forests" than Fr. Louis and his many novices.

Thus, in the "line of his duty," he would have free, legitimate, and "obedience blessed" access to the woods at any time.

When he came for his usual weekly visit, I told him of the decision; I also told him that I would write all the details to the Visitor, and explain it to the Community so that all would understand. What happiness and gratitude beamed from his eyes! The Visitor understood the situation perfectly and approved it.

Just how did Fr. Louis become Master of Novices? The State Forestry Department of Kentucky wanted to erect a very tall "Fire Tower" on one of our highest ridges, or "knobs," as they are called locally. We gave them permission. The Tower was part of a system of towers erected to keep watch over any possible fires starting in the surrounding woodlands. The tower was made of steel with a large "cabin" on the very top. This cabin had glass windows on all sides. Inside was a telephone and short wave radio. When the Warden spotted a fire, he communicated with several other Fire Towers miles away. The fire thus could be "pin-pointed" exactly, and the fire fighters rushed to the exact spot.

The view from this tower was fantastic. During its construction, Fr. Louis visited the tower and climbed up to the top. He was hypnotized by the 360 degree view of the entire surrounding woodlands.

The next day he came to see me. "Reverend Father," he said, "the Forestry Department of Kentucky will need a Fire Warden. That tower, with its trap door at the top, will be absolutely ideal for a hermitage. I could lock myself in, without any fear of intrusion. What do you say—let me give it a try."

"Well, it sounds good," I said, "but I have no authority to allow a Choir Monk to absent himself from the Divine Office in Choir. The present legislation of our Order stands against that."

Then I added: "Remember the difficulties we had about going outside the enclosure even to walk in the woods. All the more would difficulties arise about a monk living permanently in the Tower—something like St. Simon Stylites."

He laughed at that. Then said: "Look, you are going to the General Chapter in France soon. See the General. Get his permission. Then we'll be on the safe side as regards any Visitors complaining and putting both of us on 'bread and water' for a week as a penance."

"A bright idea," I replied. "You always have bright ideas. I'll see the General."

At the Chapter, I explained the situation to the General. He said: "O.K., but with this condition, that Fr. Louis be 100% hermit—that is, not be a cenobite in the morning and a hermit only in the afternoon."

"Merci beaucoup, Mon Révèrendissime Père," I said. "I'll tell Father Louis what you said." On my return from the General Chapter, Fr. Louis came at once to see me.

"The General says O.K.—provided it is a full-time life as a hermit."

Fr. Louis was radiant. "Terrific—terrific," he said. "I never expected it." Although his expressions of gratitude and delight were quite prolific, I seemed to sense that, now he was actually confronted with the reality of living alone in the tower, he was a little hesitant. However, he knew that I had done all that one in my position could do for his hermitage. Now it was up to him.

At that particular time, our Father Master assumed another position in another monastery. Thus, I needed to appoint a new Novice Master. It is a supremely important position in the Community. The future of the Community depends on the right training of the novices. As I reviewed

THE SPIRITUAL SON   151

the list of available "possibilities" for the position, I found that there were not too many who could handle the responsibilities.

Three days after my previous conversation with Fr. Louis about his "Fire Tower" hermitage life he came again to see me. "Reverend Father," he said, "you have need of a new Father Master of Novices. I've been giving it deep and prayerful thought. If you so judge, I'll be willing to take the job, and thus help you out."

My heart leapt with joy. I had had terrific misgivings about his Fire Tower project. Yet I wanted to give him every opportunity. But now Jesus had come to my rescue and had turned Fr. Louis' thoughts from the tower life to taking care of our novices.

However, I did not dare allow any of my inward relief to surface. Instead, I said, "Well, give me three days to think it over."

In three days Fr. Louis returned. "It's all right to be Father Master," I said, "but only on two conditions. One, that you'll keep the job for three years, and two, that you'll give no conferences on becoming hermits!"

At this he laughed and laughed. I laughed, also. He knew what I meant. "Don't make me take any vows on this," he said, "I've enough now. But I do promise to do as you say." This appointment seemed to lift a tremendous load off his heart.

Fr. Louis was an excellent Master of Novices. He put his whole heart and soul into his work. He worked together with me in trying to solve various difficult cases that would arise. When I was away on trips of Visitations to our Daughter Houses, he always wrote letters to keep me up-to-date. He would always add a few words about himself. For example, he ended one letter: "As for the Novice Master—I can't complain. Things are good and peaceful, time for reading, and prayer, and work in the woods. Time to think of the goodness of God, and of His Wisdom and Mercy, and to feel surrounded in His love and immersed in it on all sides. I mean in a quiet, dry sort of way, without enthusiasms, and without excesses.

"The way I travel has always been dark and fairly desolate, because my road is lonely, and I know that it is supposed to be that way—in spite of the exterior fuss and noise that people make about me. That is all past and over—or soon will be anyway. Remember me to everyone on the Foundations. Please pray for me, and give me your blessing, and to the novices, also. They all pray for you and send their love. Your devoted son in Jesus."

During the twenty years we lived together, he never missed a week in coming over to the office to converse with me. This was true not only when he held an office in the Community, such as Master of the Students, and later as Master of Novices, but also when he held no particular office. During the last fifteen years, he was my Confessor. Sometimes during Confession, our conversation would wander to extrinsic problems. Some five or ten minutes would pass, without either of us being aware of it. Suddenly, he would cry out: "Hey, Reverend Father, let me give you Absolution, and get you off your knees."

To which I would reply, "O.K., but first soak me with a good penance for being such a tough old Superior." He never would.

Knowing my great inclination toward, and preference for, greater silence, solitude, and seclusion with Jesus, Fr. Louis always encouraged me. Some thirteen years ago, on his urging, he had me set aside Wednesday completely as a Day of Recollection in the literal sense of that word. Fr. Prior was the First Superior for that day and tended to all the business and permissions. Regularly, weather permitting, I would spend the time tramping through our wonderful forests, fields, and farms.

It was with his counsel, advice, and approval that in 1968 I finally saw my way clear to follow Jesus' call to a "vocation within a vocation" and live a complete hermit life on the property of the monastery—some six miles away. But Jesus had kept me waiting some forty years before He finally said, "Come."

Previously in 1965, after Fr. Louis had been Master of Novices for some ten years, he came to me and said: "Reverend Father, I've been Master now since 1955. Isn't it about time that I live the hermit life over there near the old sheep barn?"

"You certainly have been most faithful as Father Master," I said. "It's O.K. with me to try your hermit life." Thus, on August 20, 1965, Fr. Louis began his hermit life in a cinderblock cabin designed by him on a wooded hill not far from the monastery.

Three years later, in September of 1968, he started on his Asian trip—a trip about which he had long dreamed, even as a hermit. However, it seemed that Jesus wanted him to wait awhile. A month after his departure I wrote him:

"Now for a more personal note, dear Fr. Louis. In my own life, I look back on the several times when I presented to my various superiors my persistent and burning inclination to a life of greater silence and solitude. Each time their answer was 'no.'

"My first reaction was to lean toward harsh and uncharitable thoughts in their regard, and even to question their motivations. But how wrong I would have been. Indeed to all outward appearances, it seemed that they were unjust and narrow. But looking through and beyond and above the appearances, they were merely instruments whom God was using to convey His will to me at that time.

"The inclination to a life of greater solitude in me was indeed from God. But the *time* for its execution had not yet come. For me, it was to wait humbly, silently, abandoned to Him. Thus I did wait—and wait—and wait. I had practically given up all hope of any fulfillment of that vocation.

"But see—at last God's time did come. He has given me silence, solitude, and seclusion far beyond my 'wildest dream'— because I waited for Him.

"So in your own regard, dear Fr. Louis, I would not be in the least surprised if at times I have indeed appeared as your 'public enemy No. 1'—your 'bête noire'—your haunting 'nemesis.' But in reality, I am not so.

"You never had—nor will you ever have—one who has been a more faithful and loyal friend and brother than myself. I never had any other motive in any decisions in your regard than your best—not necessarily your best temporal interests—but your best eternal interests. As Psalm 76 phrases it: 'And I had in mind the Eternal Years'—'et annos aeternos, in mente habui.'

"In the face of crosses, crises, and under the pressure of trials and frustrations of past years, whether on the part of others or of myself, I always admired your basic faith in God and your ultimate humility.

"For example, in regard to your present trip to the Orient which you desired for several years, and for which you did not receive permission, I was only an instrument in God's hands. God's time for it had not come.

"Now His time has come. You will see that the fruits which you will reap from it—for yourself and for others—will be far more abundant, lasting, and beyond your expectations. Why?—because you waited for God!

"Be assured that my poor prayers, sacrifices, and midnight Masses in Calvary Hermitage will follow you every inch of the trip until you return to us again."

I never dreamed how the fruits of the trip, for him, would be so "abundant, lasting and beyond your expectations"—namely, Heaven itself. Certainly, Heaven and the Beatific Vision is "abundant and lasting" beyond our wildest imaginings! (St. Paul)

Fr. Louis wrote me in reply from Calcutta, as follows: "I have been waiting for a chance to thank you for your warm and gracious letter. I want you to know that I appreciate it. Certainly, you must not feel that I failed to understand the situation.

"Personally, I never resented any of your decisions, because I knew you were following your conscience and the policies that seemed necessary then.

"This trip is a hard one. So far every move here has been

very quiet. I have avoided people who might make a fuss over me . . . I don't anticipate any publicity problems in Asia.

"Be sure, that I have never changed in my respect for you as Abbot, and affection as Father. Our different views certainly did not affect our deep agreement on the real point of life and of our vocation.

"I hope you are enjoying a beautiful quiet Autumn out in the wild knobs of Kentucky."

Little did he realize that within less than two months his strange and unique manner of leaving this world would become an affair of international concern.

There is one point that sometimes appears in articles about Fr. Louis. It is not a little amusing to me to read: "Evidently, the superior had Fr. Louis chained to a typewriter to keep on turning out articles, prefaces, periodicals, poems, books, and so forth."

Indeed, the contrary is true. Fr. Louis had maximum freedom within the bosom of our cloistered family in all particulars. In fact some of the monks complained to the Visitor that I allowed Fr. Louis to do just about as he pleased. However, realizing that Fr. Louis was not an average person, but more in the line of genius, I allowed him what one would call "exceptions" to various rules.

Thus in regard to his writings, he was perfectly free to write, or not to write at all. He was free to write whatever he wanted. Plainly, he had a real compulsion to write.

Once he said to me: "I am most grateful that you put no obstacles to my writing. If ever I were forbidden to write, I would soon land in a mental hospital."

Indeed, I never asked him to write any single thing except on one occasion. Several years ago a friend was helping to prepare the Papal Pavilion for the World's Fair in New York. He asked me if I would have Fr. Louis compose an appropriate prayer for a souvenir card for all those who would visit the Pavilion.

Fr. Louis graciously complied, and the prayer was published. A copy is included at the end of this letter. All the rest of his voluminous writings are his own individual works.

Another point which one or two writers have mentioned is also quite amusing: It is said that Fr. Louis had been elected as Abbot of a small monastery, but that his own Superior refused to allow him to accept. Although he was popular enough to have been elected an Abbot, this never happened.

The truth of the matter is as follows. Some fifteen years ago, I said to him: "Some day, one of our foundations may elect you as Abbot. What think you?"

"Oh, never," he said. "I am positively opposed to such a position. I am simply not cut out for that job, either by temperament, character, aptitude, or desire. 'Nix' for me. It is simply not my vocation. Besides, I have a special reason never to accept."

He told me the reason, which was serious enough. "But in the emotional enthusiasm of the moment, you might forget all this and accept," I said.

"No," said Fr. Louis, "I'll take a vow to God, right now, in your presence, never to accept." And he did.

Later it happened, in a couple of our monasteries, that Fr. Louis was seriously considered as a candidate for Abbot by some of the monks. Thus it had to be explained that it was useless to cast a vote for him, since he had made a serious vow never to accept under any circumstances.

Even in January 1968, before the election of the one who would succeed me at Gethsemani, Fr. Louis passed around a paper, instructing everyone not to "waste" a vote on him since he would not accept.

In regard to the circumstances of his death, a monk said to me: "You know there are two ironies of fate in regard to Fr. Louis' passing away which are quite intriguing."

"What are they?" I asked.

"Remember how Fr. Louis used to inveigh against machines—the monster machines. Yet, it was the big electric fan really that caused his death.

"The other irony of fate is even more striking. He was always writing against the military complex—of all branches of the Service. Yet, it was the U.S. Army officials who took charge of his body in Bangkok, provided the embalming and coffin, and then in a U.S. Air Force plane flew the body all the way to a California airport."

"True enough," I said. "I'll wager Fr. Louis had a good laugh in Heaven at all this."

Later, I met another person who had known Fr. Louis in his Columbia and New York days. He spoke to me after the burial services about several things concerning Fr. Louis. Finally he said: "When one considers Fr. Louis, what a hectic career he had before entering Gethsemani. He was so highly individualistic. He was not of a pietistic stereotype. He was also quite precipitous in his actions, and almost whimsical in changing original plans. Yet he persevered in his Trappist vocation for twenty-seven years and in his vows as a member of Gethsemani—that is what I call a first-class miracle of grace."

I replied simply: "Yes, a miracle of grace, indeed. But also, he did correspond with that grace."

Fr. Louis had been very enthusiastic about the "League for Priestly Adoration" and had become a very intimate friend of both Cardinal Roberti and Archbishop Carinci. On learning of Fr. Louis' death, Cardinal Roberti wrote from Rome:

"The very fact of his passing away in these days of special concentration on problems regarding expanding bonds of Brotherhood in the monastic fields, even with special souls who are non-Christian, makes us think that God has accepted his holocaust for the illuminating of such souls, with the Light of Christ. Souls like Fr. Louis have no need whatsoever of purification, and preparation for death, which sickness usually provides. They have to answer to Jesus' announcement: 'Behold I come quickly—Etiam venio cito'— merely: 'Come—Lord Jesus—Veni, Domine Jesu.'"

In 1948 when he published the Epilogue of *The Seven Storey Mountain*, little did he dream how true in regard to his death would be the words he had Our Lord say to him:

Everything that touches you shall *burn you.*
Do not ask when it will be,
or where it will be

or how it will be.
On a mountain or in a prison
or in a desert or in a concentration camp
or in a hospital or at Gethsemani.
It does not matter.
So do not ask me, because I am not going to tell you.
You will not know, until you are in it.
But you shall taste the true solitude of My anguish
      and of My Poverty.
I shall lead you into high places of My joy and you
      shall die in Me.
And find all things in My Mercy, which has created
      you for this end . . .
that you may become the brother of God.
And learn to know the Christ of the *burnt men.*

How prophetic the Epilogue was. After all, electricity is fire. He was burnt. Also, he was all alone in his room—true solitude, true poverty.

Certainly, we are sure, Jesus took Fr. Louis at the peak of Fr. Louis' union with Him. It sweetens our sorrow, and even gives a supernatural joy to know that he is safe for all eternity —the "sine qua non," i.e., the essential goal of all living for any one of us, for everyone of us.

Recently, I came across an ordination souvenir card of Fr. Louis. The text he then chose in 1949 was also very apropos. It was taken from Genesis, Chapter V, verse 24, in regard to Enoch. It read: "He walked with God, and was seen no more because God took him."

May all of us be equally ready when Jesus will call us— because we know "not the day nor the hour"—"neque diem neque horam."

As for Fr. Louis, so it could be for anyone of us, that, "The coming of the Son of Man will be like lightning."

But the most sublime and consoling sentence in his remarkably prophetic Epilogue mentioned above was Jesus' prediction: "You shall die in ME."

Fr. M. James, O.C.S.O.

P.S. Below is the prayer which Fr. Louis composed for the Vatican Pavilion of the World's Fair in New York (1964–1965) and which was published on the reverse of the photo of Michelangelo's *Pieta:*

"O God of mercy and of truth, look down we beg You upon this troubled world, and grant the light of Your grace to all who are kept by ignorance or scandal from coming to the knowledge of Your Truth. Grant all men light to see You, by faith, in Your Holy Church, the Mystical Body of Your Divine Son. Grant us, members of that Mystical Body, to live worthily and gratefully, and grant us a better understanding of our supernatural vocation, and of the responsibilities it entails. If by our infidelities we are concealing Your Truth instead of revealing it to other men, grant that we too may receive light and strength to be completely renewed in the love of Christ and of His Church, and grant that all men may come to unity in faith, worship and obedience, to Your holy Will, that our world may receive the gift of peace and salvation. Through the same Christ, Our Lord, Amen."

ALDHELM CAMERON-BROWN

ZEN MASTER

A Zen master said to his disciple: "Go get my
    rhinoceros horn fan."
DISCIPLE: "Sorry, Master, it is broken."
MASTER: "Okay, then get me the rhinoceros."
(A Zen *mondo* from *Zen and the Birds of Appetite*)

Thomas Merton must have known of those Zen masters who
knew (as some of the Christian saints have known) when
they were going to die. Such a man would gather his friends
together as the hour approached. He would perform some
last act, such as writing a poem or making a flower arrangement as he sat with his friends around him. Then he would
compose himself, and enter into a state of meditation from
which he never emerged.

But there is another type of Zen death. It occurs when a
man stays in one monastery for over twenty-five years, hardly
ever leaving it except for a very occasional visit to the nearest
town, and then at last travels half way round the world, to
die suddenly on foreign soil. Merton himself would have
laughed at the absurdity of such a death; indeed, he is probably laughing now. But for us who are left, a prophet departed
from Israel.

A whole generation of monks entered the cloister in an atmosphere engendered, at least in part, by *The Seven Storey
Mountain,* that swan song of the nineteenth-century monastic revival. At the time it was published, it was also a siren
song, and in some Benedictine novitiates Merton was forbidden reading: he was too apt to give the young monks "Cister-

cian fever." Today, of course, the novice master who has the good fortune to have any novices at all has quite the opposite problem: how to stop them running off to the nearest town and setting up a monastic life in the slums and factories. But if novices have changed, so did Merton, though not quite in the same direction; and if in the monastic order one age is dying while another seems (as yet) powerless to be born, Merton was at least doing his best to act as midwife.

There are many writers who have approached monastic renewal as the rediscovery of community life, of community as communion; and here is a region where contemporary thought has really new and essential insights to offer to monastic life. Father Merton has shown himself aware of this aspect (for example, in *Zen and the Birds of Appetite*, p. 30), but he was not primarily concerned with it. Rather, his work is especially valuable because he was one of the few writers really trying to express the "mystical"—or better, "sapiential" —aspect of monasticism *in modern terms*. Which aspect appeals to a man most is probably largely a matter of temperament. They are complementary, and certainly a discovery of community is essential for a really deep contemplative life, and will lead to it. If it is not often referred to in Merton's writings, that is compensated by the importance of his strong points, and their comparative neglect elsewhere.

The Seven Storey Mountain is a difficult book to read right through today, though it still has passages where one feels the old magic. There is the ludicrous account of Cambridge as a kind of diabolical morass (Merton's attitude to England was usually perverse, though he tries to make some amends in *Conjectures*); but there is also the account of Harlem, which lives and takes fire because it is informed with Merton's characteristic compassion.

Then there are the passages where *fuga mundi* (flight from the world) is carried to an extreme. "Behind the monastery was a dark curtain of woods, and over to the west was a wooded valley, and beyond that a rampart of wooded hills, a barrier and a defense against the world" (p. 320). And Cistercians for the young Merton had the advantage over the

Carthusians, in that the latter had a recreation period once a week, in which they actually spoke.

But against all this there is a hunger and thirst, a passion for God, which one rarely finds expressed nowadays. Indeed, people would perhaps be embarrassed to admit such a thing, lest they be suspected of neglecting God as He is to be found in our neighbor (or lest they be asked to explain what they mean by God). Many Christians today hunger and thirst after social justice; many nonbelievers also thirst after social justice, and in doing so undoubtedly contact God. But that is not the only way of apprehending him (or being apprehended by him), nor is it the most basic. My neighbor is indeed an icon of God; but then, so is my self, in a different way or, rather, offering a different approach.

If it comes to that, Thomas Merton also fought for social justice, in his way. Social questions had involved him even in his earlier days (see entry for September 1, 1941, in *A Secular Journal*); they were not just a mark of the new Merton. But now as a monk, in spite of his *fuga mundi*, he showed that even the most contemplative monk may (must?) be concerned with the needs of the world, that his prayer will be all the keener if he feels the anguish of the world. And all the more so today when the monk (in most cases) does not experience that anguish by material poverty and insecurity in his own life. Merton was possibly the only writer at all favored by the Establishment to write regularly for the *Catholic Worker*, and English readers will remember his biting analysis of the "liberal" attitude to race problems in the old *Blackfriars* at the beginning of this decade. It was in *Blackfriars*, too, that he was saying, before Vatican II, that Christian missionary work would be more effective if the missionary approached men of other religions with an attempt to discover Christ already present in their beliefs, in a hidden manner, rather than by thinking of themselves as bringing Christ to the unenlightened heathen. As a monk, Merton was able to write on social topics with a detachment and truth sometimes difficult for those in the field, where compromise inevitably creeps in or is avoided only by erecting a sterilizing hatred.

But all this was, so to speak, the overflow of Merton's main activity of prayer. And if this comes out (sometimes rather self-consciously) in *The Seven Storey Mountain*, it does so much more strongly in *The Sign of Jonas*, which strikes one today as being much less outmoded in its attitudes, and in its last section reaches heights which, in that field, he never surpassed. And here, of course, was one of Merton's great dangers from the novice master's point of view: he had a natural facility in prayer. The novice would read of him flopping down behind a pillar for half an hour's thanksgiving after Mass; then, finding that for himself (as for most people) the period after Mass is the most difficult of all during the day in which to pray, even for ten minutes, finding that his prayer anyhow never at any time resembled the descriptions of Merton's prayer, he would conclude that the life of prayer was not for him, or (perhaps more often) that his own particular monastery just did not provide the right conditions for it. This situation was a little eased when Merton conceded, in *The Silent Life*, that even Benedictines could be contemplatives.

Thomas Merton's outlook expanded, however. In both *The Sign of Jonas* and *Conjectures* he describes how he went in to Louisville and suddenly realized that the people there were not just "the wicked world." "Perhaps the things I had resented about the world when I left it were defects of my own that I had projected upon it. Now, on the contrary, I found that everything stirred me with a deep and mute sense of compassion" (*Jonas*, p. 91). "I was suddenly overwhelmed with the realization that I loved all those people. . . . The whole illusion of a separate holy existence is a dream. Not that I question the reality of my vocation, or of my monastic life: but the conception of 'separation from the world' that we have in the monastery too easily presents itself as a complete illusion: the illusion that by making vows we become a different species of being, pseudo-angels, 'spiritual men,' men of interior life, what have you" (*Conjectures*, pp. 140–41).

Probably most monks can testify that this attitude has existed in the past, at least implicitly. Whereas the truth is, as Merton had already explained (*Jonas*, p. 273): "To penetrate the truth of how utterly unimportant we are is the only thing that can set us free to enjoy true happiness." That, of course, is what St. Benedict is trying to express in the seventh degree of humility. "The source of all sorrow is the illusion that of ourselves we are anything but dust. God is all our joy, and in Him our dust can become splendor" (*Jonas*, p. 279).

Although, as we saw, Merton did not write much on community values, this sense of identification with all men and compassion with them was there, and sometimes comes through very strongly in his writings, as, for instance, in the extraordinary passage in *Conjectures* (p. 193) where he goes into the empty novitiate scriptorium at night. Everything that the novices can be said to "possess"—a few letters and so on—is in their desks in this empty room. And so, "it seemed that, because all that they loved was there, 'they' in a spiritual way were most truly there, though in fact they were upstairs in the dormitory asleep. It was as if their love and their goodness had transformed the room and filled it with a presence curiously real, comforting, perfect: one might say, with Christ. Indeed, it seemed to me momentarily that he was as truly present here, in a certain way, as upstairs in the chapel." And he says further down the page: "You can see the beauty of Christ in each individual person, in that which is most his, most human, most personal to him, in things which an ascetic might advise you sternly to get rid of."

But if Merton, in spite of such passages, was principally occupied with prayer, here too he changed; and an indication of the change can be seen by comparing *Seeds of Contemplation* with *New Seeds of Contemplation*, a book which is one of the few works of this century which really may deserve to become a "spiritual classic." At first glance, *New Seeds* is simply a revision of *Seeds*. But the alterations and additions are revealing.

To start with, there are the chapters at the beginning of *New Seeds* in which Merton says something about what contemplation is and also (very much to the point) what it is not. Then on page 25 there is a long passage, absent from *Seeds*, emphasizing our own part in the creation of our "true selves." The *fuga mundi* passages are toned down in the later book, and while both works relate contemplation to fraternal charity, this is brought out more strongly in *New Seeds*. There is much more in the later book on faith, and how it brings a new element into our lives; and also much more on war. Both books are notable in relating mysticism to Christ (so many books on prayer appear to be only superficially Christian); and both books contain one of the finest passages written about Our Lady in modern times. In Merton's later books, the frequent prayers to Mary, rather self-consciously addressing her simply as "Lady," disappear; but it is evident from this passage that his union with her had become deeper, and therefore silent.

But more significantly, *New Seeds* expands the final chapter of the earlier book with a long passage on the "true" and the "false" self; Merton explains, too, that the false self is emphatically not to be equated with the body. Then follows a completely new chapter on the general dance of creation, and a suspicion which has been growing throughout the book is verified right at the end, when Basho's frog plops onto the last page, and we realize that Thomas Merton has come under the influence of Zen.

His writings henceforth coruscate with "Zen flashes in the heart of the Church," as he puts it in *Conjectures*. There is in that book, for example, the beautiful passage on the dawn (p. 117). But besides these flashes, there were now whole books and articles on Zen.

Thomas Merton was not a first-class original thinker; but he had read very widely (how did he find time for it, in a monastery; and how did he take it all in?), and on top of this his lived experience as a mystic gave him an authority in this field which he had in no other, although he was quite a capable "popularizer" of, say, modern philosophical ideas. It was probably this experience which enabled him to enter into the ideas and life of Buddhism to an extent possibly unequaled by other contemporary Catholic writers on the subject. The fruits of this are evident in two of his latest books, *Mystics and Zen Masters* and the remarkable *Zen and the Birds of Appetite*.

The significance of Buddhism for today lies in the fact that, although it has often been made a religion, it is in essence neither a religion nor a philosophy, but a way of being in the world. This applies especially to Zen; and the whole Zen approach to life is contemplative. This has its importance today when the civilization of the West is at the furthest point from the contemplative (in the essay "The New Consciousness" in *Zen and the Birds* . . . pp. 15 ff., Merton explains how this has come about), and when even within the Church contemplation and mysticism are highly suspect among those very "progressives" in whom our hope for the future of the Church (humanly speaking) lies. It is little wonder that so many people today, disillusioned with the materialism and self centered attitude of the modern world, feel that the Church is too much a part of that world and turn to exiled Tibetan lamas for spiritual direction.

Many of the Zen masters were recluses and lived in remote sites, and their nearness to nature influenced the Japanese a great deal; nevertheless, Zen does not depend on a flight from the world of men and cities. Indeed, the Japanese, whose national character is very much moulded by Buddhism among other influences, are remarkable for the way they have learned to preserve calm and tranquility in the midst of some of the noisiest and most crowded cities in the world. This in itself suggests that Zen might be as influential in the contemplative life of the twentieth century as Platonism was to earlier Christian monks. There will always be a need for monasteries which withdraw into the wilderness, but it may well be that in the future there will also be monasteries set in an urban milieu (indeed, can one really deny the title of "monk" to the Little Brothers and Sisters of Jesus and their companion orders?) and even for those monks who live in the desert, there is an urgent need that they should be able to teach those who come out from the cities to visit them some way of life and prayer that is both contemplative and also compatible with the daily life of a modern town. It is only fair to add that Thomas Merton himself seems to have given only a qualified approval to urban monasticism. (See the letter of Thomas Merton published in *L'Osservatore Romano*, English version, Jan. 23, 1969, p. 5.)

Zen does not conflict with Christianity, because they are not on the same plane. "Zen is not Kerygma, but realization, not revelation but consciousness, not news from the Father who sent his Son into this world, but awareness of the ontological ground of our own being here and now, right in the midst of this world" (*Zen and the Birds*, p. 47). But as Merton goes on to say, the supernatural Kerygma and the metaphysical intuition of the ground of being are far from being incompatible. One may be said to prepare the way for the other.

Merton had met Dr. Daisetz Suzuki, who (as he says) "contributed no little to the spiritual and intellectual revolution of our time" by bringing Zen to the West, and he was immensely impressed by him. Suzuki used to say that Zen is not mysticism; at any rate, they certainly have much in common, and, as Suzuki shows in his own contribution to *Zen and the Birds of Appetite*, Zen "emptiness" is very like Christian "poverty of spirit"; and the Zen master compares the Zen *prajna* or "wisdom" to the innocence of Adam before the Fall in the Genesis story. Since Merton was thoroughly steeped in the writings of the Fathers of the Church and the early Cistercian Fathers, who were fond of the theme of the "return to Paradise" and the recovery of the image of God in man, here was a point of contact between two representatives of two great spiritual traditions.

With all this interest in Zen, Thomas Merton never ceased to be truly a man of his own Western, Christian, and monastic tradition. He was not an uprooted Westerner trying to be Asiatic. Rather, he exemplified in his own person what he himself gave as the monk's most important contribution to ecumenism: to reconcile various religious and spiritual traditions in his own person. He never ceased to love the monastic

tradition in which he was brought up, even though he could
see its faults and realized that the whole tradition must pass,
or at least be considerably modified; but he was always open
to new influences and ideas, and hence could be an inspiration to others (usually younger than himself) who might be
able to refashion monastic life. There was the South American who said to him, "Why would not you, Father Merton,
leave here and come to South America and start a totally new
kind of monastic order, one that would appeal more to men
of modern times?" He comments: "I could not tell him how
much I would like to try it, or how impossible it would be to
make any such attempt without leaving the Order, and how
impossible it would be for me to try to leave the Order"
(*Conjectures*, p. 144). And one reason that it was impossible
was, of course, that he loved it. After his death, the *Catholic
Worker* repaid his faithfulness as a contributor by scotching
the many rumors that Merton intended to leave (or had actually left) his monastery. Dorothy Day personally wrote his
obituary and included extracts from some letters of his to
her. "I have had enough experience in 24 years of monastic
life to know that even if certain measures of superiors may be
a little unfair, one never loses anything by obeying, quite the
contrary." He writes of his "trying to live an authentic life of
solitude (which I certainly think will do more for the peace
movement than anything I write). . . . I am more determined than ever on my present course" (*Catholic Worker*,
December, 1968, p. 6).

It was, perhaps, the combined influence of the Cistercian
Fathers and of Zen which led to the outlook on monastic life
which Thomas Merton expressed in two of the latest and
most remarkable articles of his life. In these, monastic life is
seen as leading equally to contemplative union with God and
to the fullest development of the monk as a human person.
Merton would perhaps have said of monastic life what J. S.
Bach said of music, that it is for the glorification of God and
the re-creation of man. These two articles were "Ecumenism
and Monastic Renewal" and "Final Integration: Toward a
Monastic Therapy." (His article in *Monastic Studies*, number

4, "Monastic Vocation and Modern Thought," was also outstanding among his several articles for this periodical.)*

In the first of these, Merton wrote: "The fundamental purpose of all monastic life is . . . to deliver the individual and the charismatic community from the massive automatic functioning of a social machine that leaves nothing to peculiar talent, to chance, or to grace. The monastic vocation calls a man to desert frontiers, beyond which there are no police, in order to dip into the 'ocean of unexploited forces which surrounds a well-ordered society and draw from it a personal provision' of grace and vision." Of course, as he adds, "the historical fate of monasticism is . . . that it has become more organized and better policed than secular society itself, and while continuing to offer promises of charismatic vision and liberty it has in fact subjected its disciples to all the most banal monotonies of an unimaginative ecclesiastical bureaucracy." This article presents one of the most penetrating analyses of the faults of monasticism as it has developed up to today that one has seen anywhere, summed up, perhaps, in the sentence: "Fidelity to tedious but predictable rule can become an easy substitute for fidelity, in openness and risk, to the unpredictable word." Merton then sketches out how he thinks monasticism might develop in the future. Amongst other things, monks in permanent vows might be only the nucleus in a community.

Thomas Merton never ceased to lay emphasis on such traditional features of monastic life as silence, solitude, and penance, though modified to take account of contemporary insights into the nature of communication and human relationships. But in these two articles in addition to all his other writings, he went perhaps more to the heart of monastic renewal than those many writers who seem to see renewal *merely* in terms of shorter office, more *lectio divina,* and dialogue with superiors, or who see "openness to the world" as meaning a life lived fully *in* the world. The difficulties in the

* These articles were later published in *Contemplation in a World of Action.*—EDITOR.

way of realizing true renewal are immense, of course, as Merton realized; not the least being that all of us are, on the whole, groping in the dark, grateful for just such light as people like him can give. But a greater difficulty is mentioned by Merton himself in the letter published in *L'Osservatore Romano*. There he says that people must find in monasteries "both a *monastic* reality (simple and deep persons who have acquired monastic values by putting them into practice), and an opening to the *social* reality of the twentieth century. It is possible that one or other of these values may be realized in our present structures. *It is very difficult for both of them to be realized at the same time.* If both of them are to be realized, the present monastic structures must be changed. The survival of monasticism requires that both should be realized."

And if monasticism does survive (as it undoubtedly will, if the Holy Spirit is still with the Church) the form it takes may well owe much to Thomas Merton.

Tarcisius Conner

MONK OF RENEWAL

Most would agree that Thomas Merton's influence upon renewal in monasticism extends beyond the usage of the term current since Vatican II. He was one of the first (at least in this country) to situate the Trappist Order within a context which was larger than merely La Trappe, and to show the historical, spiritual, and theological areas of contact with monasticism in general. He was a trail-blazer in seeing that the basis of the Cistercian life goes beyond merely the Usages and Constitutions, and that our roots are still deeply embedded in the early monasticism of Anthony, Pachomius, Basil, and Benedict. He saw the relationship which exists between our Cistercian Fathers and the Greek Fathers of the Church even before Gilson, Bouyer, and others had popularized this. He accentuated the fact that Cistercian spirituality must be broader than simply a life of penance, that it must be centered in the one quality which St. Benedict saw as essential to the monk: an ultimate search for God in a life which favors prayer and meditation.

It can only be seen as unfortunate that Fr. Louis was not more actively involved in the practical implementation of renewal within the Order, through the General Chapters, regional meetings, etc. The reasons for this lack of involvement are many and complex, both on his own part and on that of the Order. At the same time, though, it is typical of Fr. Louis that his influence was asserted more on the level of the ordinary monk since, he had more confidence in a renewal which comes from below than one which is imposed from above.

While the major superiors and the competent Councils and Chapters must of course finally decide what adaptations are to be put into effect, in accordance with the Rule and Constitutions, it is nevertheless essential that all the members should actively participate in such tasks as: estimation of the meaning and value of their vocation, clarification of the relevance of their particular religious ideal for themselves and their time, evaluation of the contribution they might make to the understanding and aid of the contemporary world, defining the relevance in a present-day context of certain observances belonging to the past, and bringing to the attention of Superiors the real everyday needs and problems of subjects.

This approach to the renewal of religious life is not merely pragmatic: it has serious theological implications, which are in accord with the new perspectives on the Church. They recognize that all true renewal must be the work of the Holy Spirit and that the Holy Spirit cannot be said to work exclusively "from the top down," manifesting the will of God only to higher superiors and, further down, granting to subjects no light but only the strength and grace to accept this will, as it comes down the chain of command, with total obedience and blind faith. The new emphasis in the theology of the Church sees the Holy Spirit working *in the collective and "collegial" effort of all*, each in his own sphere and according to his own function in the Church. (*The Council and Monasticism*, March, 1965, p. 10)

When one comes to his actual thought on renewal, one finds himself faced with something which is so complex and so varied that it is almost impossible to grasp in its entirety. It has been frequently pointed out that he was a man of apparent contradictions. He would often make some point, only later to assert what appeared to be diametrically opposed. This has been explained in part by the fact that he was more intuitive than reflective; more of a mystic or prophet than a philosopher or sociologist. And yet this does not mean that his thought has not been expressed in clear and concise terms. It merely indicates that his thought was always fragmentary and always "historical," in the sense that it was always centered upon that portion of reality which he was confronting, even though it still retained, at least in his own mind, a definite relationship with what had gone before and what was yet to come. But because his own personality was so dynamic and so enthusiastic, he tended to give the impression that what he said in each case was an adequate expression of the matter at hand. In actual fact, when this was pointed out to him, he himself would be the first to say that there were many other elements which should be considered besides what he had said in this particular context. It had to be modified by what might be said on the same subject in other contexts and what might be said on other subjects in relation to this.

This is nowhere more true than in the matter of renewal—whether this pertains to renewal within the Church at large or renewal within the context of monasticism. Fr. Louis was a firm believer in renewal and frequently spoke of it. He made a distinction between renewal and reform: "Renewal is something deeper and more total than reform. Reform was proper to the needs of the Church at the time of the Council of Trent, where the whole structure of religious life had collapsed, even though there was still a great deal of vitality among religious. Today the structure and organization is firm and intact: what is lacking is a deep and fruitful understanding of the real meaning of religious life" (*ibid.* p. 8).

He defined this renewal as: "a restoration of authentic meaning to forms and acts that must recover their full value as sacred signs" (*ibid.* p. 14). Yet this did not mean for him that renewal was merely a question of semantics or verbalization. Here again, though, his thought tended to appear as contradictory. In one place he would speak of the current renewal as being a "collapse of formal structures that were no longer properly understood; a repudiation of genuine tradition, discipline, contemplation, trivializing the monastic life"; and he would attribute this to an "obsession with *relevance* to the new generation" (Calcutta conference). He would harshly criticize this, saying: "In the West there is now going on a great upheaval in monasticism, and much that is of undying value is being thrown away irresponsibly, foolishly, and they are accepting things that are showy, that have no ultimate value" (Calcutta talk). This might seem to indicate that he was in favor of simply conserving the things of the past, while revitalizing their meaning. But such is not the case, for in another place he says: "Certain structures need to be shaken, certain structures have to fall. We need not be revolutionaries within our institutions. . . . But on the other hand, we don't want to go to the other extreme and just simply be ostriches refusing to see that these institutions are in many respects outdated, and that perhaps renewal may mean the collapse of some institutional structures and starting over again with a whole new form" ("Is the 'Contemplative Life' Finished?," *Monastic Studies*, Vol. 7).

Likewise when speaking to the novice masters of the Order, he said: "The conservative element is convinced that the *only* monasticism for us is the kind that we have always had and that this cannot be changed; that the only thing we can do about it is dress it up a little, patch it a little. With this view, there can be no serious development of monasticism. If that view prevails, then monasticism will soon be dead in the Cistercian Order. There will be no future. So there has to be real change" (Notes of the Meeting of American Novice Masters, 1968).

Between these two positions we can detect the complexity of his own view. Renewal is absolutely necessary for all religious orders. Even if we had any doubt in this regard ourselves, we have been given an explicit mandate by the Vatican Council (Perfectae caritatis, no. 2, 3, 7 . . .). Yet this renewal cannot be something which destroys the Order rather than renews it. It must be related to the essentials of the life, to clarifying these and making them more accessible to those who enter. This may require change, but the emphasis is to be placed, not on change alone, but on the contemplative values which are to be regained or restored to sight.

A spirit of openness will be most important in any renewal of religious life. This means that observances which are 'closed' and incomprehensible even to the religious themselves will almost inevitably generate a spirit of pretentiousness and artificiality which is incompatible with the true Gospel simplicity. Such observances must either be re-thought so that they recover a living meaning, or they must be discarded, and if necessary replaced by others that fulfill the function which they have ceased to fulfill. ("The Council and Monasticism," p. 14)

Consequently what is basically needed is an openness to the Spirit, a spirit of detachment, by which one can approach all monastic observances with a freedom of heart to discern whether they are fulfilling their purpose or not. The monk has to be one who places his hope in God alone, rather than in any particular ritual way of life. He has to be willing to seek "God alone" and to drop anything which will not truly assist in this search. This very willingness indicates the extent to which the monk has a true faith in his monastic vocation, or to what extent he is basing his faith on an observance of "works."

"We do not come here to be transformed by our own will and our own spirit. We come here to make this complete surrender in faith. Whether we go by the old way or by the new way, this faith is radically and urgently and critically the most important thing" ("Is the 'Contemplative Life' Finished?," p. 62). It is precisely this spirit of faith which will give us true discernment as to the changes to be made. To hold rigidly to either extreme, whether that of change or of conservatism, will be fatal for the monastic vocation.

Let us admit that quite possibly if we are too ready to sacrifice silence, solitude, etc., we may quickly find ourselves deserted by vocations. [But also] if by relinquishing my own favorite interpretation of what the perfect life of silence and contemplation ought to be and submitting to certain adaptations I can make the monastic life possible for others who would not otherwise be able to live it, then it would seem that charity itself ought to tell me that this "need" of others is an appeal to my own generosity, in a way very different from that which I anticipated when I made my vows. Let us recall that precisely such generosity as this characterized St. Benedict. ("Monastic Attitudes," *Cistercian Studies*, 1967, p. 13)

Consequently we can see that what at first appeared to be a contradiction in Merton's thought is in actual fact an application of his thought to each of the two opposite poles within renewal. Depending on whether he is referring to those who are too eager to change or to those who are unyielding to change, his thought takes on different expression. But in itself, his thought attempts to avoid precisely that polarization which would be detrimental to renewal and would even lead to a loss of the monastic ideal itself.

This polarization can best be avoided if the monk clearly recalls that his life is ultimately based on the experience of the act of faith. This faith means that the monk is called to depend solely upon God Himself and that all exterior realities have to be an expression of this faith rather than a substitution for it. Yet it is precisely this which is most difficult. For, as Fr. Louis wrote in a letter to a brother monk: "At root we are men of very little faith; and though we claim to believe in the Risen Savior, at heart we have more faith in forms and formulas and systems." It is this lack of faith which forms the gravest temptation for the monk who tends to base his monasticism on the exterior forms it takes. He saw that it was this mistake which brought on the crisis for Martin Luther. "Luther's 'monastic' experience was in fact quite central to his whole view of the Church and Christian life, and his repudiation of religious vows was a critical point in his theology of *fides sola*" ("Ecumenism and Monastic Renewal," p. 1). In actual fact, such a crisis was not called for. Monasticism, rightly understood, is likewise an expression of the true Pauline "*fides sola*" and any exterior practice is seen to be beneficial only to the extent that it springs from, and is an expression of, this Faith.

Accordingly certain practices of monastic life may tend to weigh down the spirit of man rather than promoting faith. To this extent, the monk must make a basic reconsideration of what his life is.

The problem of monastic renewal, at the deepest level, is theological and it is at this point that the monks are finally coming face to face with Luther's challenge. In "returning to the sources" they are only doing in a more thorough and systematic way what Luther himself did by reexamining his vocation in the light of the Gospel and the Pauline Epistles. Studying the original monastic sources, seen in their historical and cultural contexts, monks begin to ask themselves more disturbing questions than those which merely bear on meaningful observance. It is no longer just a matter of recovering a genuine understanding of monastic enclosure, silence, worship, fasting and trying to adapt these to a modern situation. The very concept of a vowed and cloistered life, of a life devoted to prayer apart from the world, of silence and asceticism, has to be reexamined. This need is realized as yet only obscurely by the majority of monks: but its nagging, disquieting presence is felt. And some of those who are now consciously aware of it are thrown into a mild panic, with the result that they are more ready to abandon ship than they are to examine carefully whether it is about to sink." (*Ibid.*)

We see here the depths to which monastic renewal must extend. For, unless the life of the monk is truly based upon faith in God alone, he will run the risk of seeing his monastic practices as an end in themselves. In this way he will either cling to them tenaciously and blindly, or else he will totally repudiate them as pure anachronisms. But in between these two extremes there is the thin line which leads to a balanced renewal, which sees the validity of the monastic vocation and which seeks to express this vocation in ways that are more consonant with man today: "It is one thing to admit that Luther had come to grips with a real problem, and another to conclude that one cannot find any other solution than his. If a ritualistic attachment to archaic observance is, indeed, theologically futile, it does not follow that monastic life cannot be lived on a deeper and more valid level. In other words, the monastic community has other choices than perpetuating an antique formula or going out of existence" (*ibid.*).

It is this "other choice" which leads to the brink of faith: faith in God and faith in the real values of monasticism. "The root of our life of metanoia is a real faith in Christ, a real faith in our vocation, a real faith in the transforming power of the Cross, a faith in God's promises, a faith that if we give up ourselves and our ambitions, even our spiritual ambitions, if we deliver ourselves utterly and totally into the hands of Christ and His Love, we will indeed be transformed in His time, in His way, by His Spirit. ("Is the 'Contemplative Life' Finished?," p. 62)

This places us squarely at the root of our renewal, which Fr. Louis sums up as "a renewal in the spheres of prayer and penance." He readily admits that we do not know exactly in what this renewal will consist. But he says that this is something which we have to discover "collectively and individually by a real cooperative search under the guidance of the Holy Spirit" (*ibid.*). It is only this *collective and individual search under the guidance of the Holy Spirit* which can avoid the danger of polarization and move forward toward renewal. This renewal, once again, must be *real*, and it must be *radical*. But it must be within the direction of the basic monastic movement. On the one hand he admits that, "if monasticism means purely and simply medieval and western monasticism, it is likely to disappear. An aggiornamento of monasticism which would be nothing more than an effort to recapture the spirit and rebuild the structures of the great medieval reforms, Cluny, Citeaux, and the rest, can result in little more than an exercise in archaism" ("The Council and Monasticism", p. 3).

Yet at the same time he emphasizes that, "the monastic past is by no means irrelevant to the problems of the present, and if the monks, in cutting themselves adrift from their medieval anchorage, simply join the convoy of active institutes, retaining only a particular communal style of life that is vaguely 'monastic' they will hardly be monks in the real sense of the word" (*ibid.*).

This immediately clarifies any reserve that Fr. Louis might express at times regarding renewal and change. He is fully convinced that, unless change comes—and that a *radical* change—monasticism will become a lost cause. Yet he is equally convinced that unless this change is guided towards the basic goals of monasticism it will likewise be the end of monasticism: "We must not go to the other extreme. The idea that we now in the monastic life or cloistered life or the contemplative life are simply throwing away all of these practices and living in a kind of freedom of spirit without any real discipline is fatal. There is no hope of any good coming out of this. It will only destroy monasticism" ("Is the 'Contemplative Life' Finished?" p. 59).

Monasticism has, as he says "a specific and precise aim" and consequently demands a certain discipline—but a discipline which is directed towards a deeper freedom. "The freedom that we are talking about in the contemplative life and in the monastic life, is the freedom which is bought by the renunciation of simple license or the simple capacity to follow any legitimate desire in any legitimate direction. Besides renouncing illegitimate freedom we also give up a certain lawful autonomy. So that we come face to face right away with the fact that the freedom we look for is bound up with restrictions" ("Is the 'Contemplative Life' Finished?," p. 34).

From this aspect, the renewal that we are seeking today is perhaps connected more with discerning which restrictions are truly necessary and helpful for the goals that we are pursuing, and which are simply an expression of something which now serves only to needlessly frustrate man.

The monastic life is not justified simply by a sort of contractual fulfillment of a "work" on behalf of the Church—even if it be the spiritual work of the "Opus Dei" or, for that matter, the cultivation of meditative prayer in silence, strict enclosure, in an austere regime. The monastic community does not effectively act as a sign of God's presence and His Kingdom merely by the fulfillment of certain symbolic functions. For instance, it is not enough to keep the monks strictly enclosed and remote from all external activity. . . . It is of course perfectly true that solitude and silence are essential to the monastic way of life and discipline does contribute very much to the ends for which the monastic communities exist. But the fact remains that people are called to the monastic life so that they may grow and be transformed, "reborn" to a new and more complete identity. When rigidity and limitation become ends in themselves they no longer favor growth, they stifle it. ("Final Integration," p. 3)

This "rebirth," which he sees as being the end of the monastic life, is elsewhere called "self-transcendence," transformation in Christ, life in the Spirit. This "transformation" is, as he says, "not a *repudiation* of ordinary life, but its definitive *recovery* in Christ." Life itself is something which, since the fall of man, is inevitably experienced only in part. But this "partial" experience can be greater or lesser according as man possesses a greater or lesser "freedom." This freedom cannot be identified with a freedom to do as one "pleases." It is a freedom to experience life as it is meant to be experienced: "The monastic charism seeks to be free from routine cares and responsibilities and claims and demands in order to be more constantly awake, alert, alive, sensitive to areas of experience which are not easily opened up in the midst of these routines which we shall call 'worldly routines'" ("Is the 'Contemplative Life' Finished?," p. 33).

This has a direct relationship with the way Merton earlier defined renewal: "a restoration of authentic meaning to forms and acts that must recover their full value as sacred signs" (cf. p. 2). The Greek Fathers, beginning with Dionysius, referred to the contemplative as one who can perceive the inner meaning of material reality. For them, all creation is a material expression of an inner spiritual reality. The contemplative strives to grasp this meaning and to order his life in relation to those external realities which best express the spiritual. It is this spirit which makes all of the exterior forms of life to be seen as "sacred signs," even as "sacraments" of the divine. In this regard, one must distinguish between "sacred signs" which, by their very nature, contain and express something of the spiritual realm, and "conventional signs" which flow from common agreement among men. Merton implies that the main elements of monastic life must be seen as pertaining to the spiritual rather than merely the sociological. It does not suffice simply to agree on the meaning or reason for doing certain things; they must be seen as bearers of the divine in fact and in reality, not only in theory. Monastic decline comes when monks are content to perform certain exterior acts merely because they are prescribed or are "customary." "Renewal" demands that the monk exert sufficient introspection to question whether the elements of his life truly bring him into newness of life.

> "On the other hand, we must not develop a sort of magic idea of the contemplative life and say that when a person puts on a certain kind of habit and gets into a certain kind of cloister and lives a certain kind of rule that automatically a deep inner kind of contemplative life follows. This is not so, and the problem of substituting cloister routines for worldly routines can really be an evasion and falsification of this call to authentic inner freedom." (*Ibid.*, p. 33)

This shows us that there is simply no exterior path which will assure that a man comes into contact with the heart of reality. And yet this contact itself is what is most essential to monasticism. "The monk is a man who, in one way or other, pushes to the very frontiers of human experience and strives to go beyond, to find out what transcends the ordinary level of existence" ("Renewal and Discipline," p. 3).

The ordinary roles which one fulfills in life by their very nature impose certain limitations on man; they "create certain limitations which hamper and frustrate a certain kind of development if we allow ourselves to remain too dependent on them" (*ibid.*). It is in order to be free from these limitations that a man seeks the monastic life.

> The monastic idea, originally, was to explore the possibilities that were opened up once these limitations were removed, that is to say, once one "left the world." . . . It was simply a question of obscurely realizing that, in some way, the limitations imposed by social life stood in the way

of something else, and the monk was one who wanted to look into this "something else." The monk is a man who, in one way or other, pushes to the very frontiers of human experience and strives to go beyond, to find out what transcends the ordinary level of existence. Aware that man is somehow sustained by a deep mystery of silence, of incomprehensibility, of God's will and God's love, the monk feels that he is personally called to live in more intimate communication with that mystery." (*Ibid.*)

This immediately sets us on the way of what is most essential in the monastic life. The monk is one who seeks to respond to the summons: "Behold, the Bridegroom comes: go out to meet Him!" and the limitations which he imposes upon himself are those which will further his watchfulness and readiness. This already gives us an insight to the question of renewal within monasticism. As Fr. Louis says, the monastic life has to become something which is thoroughly human, and yet not fall into the very limitations from which the monk is striving to be freed. Here, again, we are in a delicate middle ground. On the one hand, he shows that the monk must be fully *human* in the best sense of the word.

The basic requirement of the contemplative and cloistered life today is this: before all else, before we either indulge in asceticism or go on to quiet contemplative absorption in God, we must recognize the need to maintain healthy human atmosphere and a normal human relationship to one another and to reality in our communities. This, of course, goes without saying, but it cannot be overemphasized, it is so easily forgotten. We have to be, first of all, healthy, mature, honest, humble men and women before we can go on to be ascetics and contemplatives. This must never be forgotten and it has to be continually returned to because it is the foundation on which all the rest is built. (*Ibid.*, p. 56)

Yet, by the very fact that it is so fundamental, it is also something which must be surpassed before one can truly be a monk. "The freedom that we are looking for must never be considered a kind of mere spontaneous following of natural tendencies, innocent natural feelings, and so forth. This idea of mere personal fulfillment is not good enough" (*Ibid.*, p. 60).

For this reason, the monk accepts certain restrictions upon his natural tendencies: not merely upon those which might lead him into evil, but even those which could be useful in any other situation. And this is the reason behind the penances which he must maintain, even in a period of renewal.

> Our freedom is by no means simply a removal of obstacles which permit us to fulfill our best natural aspirations. We do not come to the cloister to become artists or musicians or to become friends with other people. We do not come to the cloister for the expansion of a merely human existence because that can be done much better somewhere else. We do not come to the cloister to find the same kind of fulfillment and expansion of our human character and personality as we would find in marriage or in a creative secular existence, a professional career in the world. We come here for a specific and precise aim, which is a special kind of transformation in Christ and a special kind of transformation in the Spirit. (*Ibid.*, p. 61)

This means that although the particular limitations or restrictions will be determined in relation to the concrete community in which one is living, yet it will not suffice to make the notion of "community" the pivotal point for renewal. Community must mean more than mere "togetherness" before it can serve the ends of the monastic life in this common pursuit to pierce the frontiers of reality. Unless it is properly used, it can cause the monk to become bogged down with the very limitations and needs which he is striving to surpass.

> Although, admittedly, if there is real charity present, if you have a real honest-to-goodness community relationship in which there is real love, certainly this will do an enormous amount; but you cannot have this without real self-denial and the problem is, of course, to what extent real love is found in these relationships? To what extent are they really love and to what extent are they mere gregari-

ousness, vapid togetherness? We cannot be content with a superficial chumminess and euphoria." (*Ibid.*, p. 60)

But, granting this pitfall as one extreme, one must also avoid the danger of minimizing the importance of community, both in this contemplative experience and in determining the concrete renewal. The very fact that, as we have already seen, renewal is a constant avoidance of two extremes requires the discernment of spirits in order that any new directions will truly be in accord with the movement of the Spirit. Monastic tradition has always placed a great deal of importance upon the abbot to fulfill this function. Now, while it remains true that the abbot still retains considerable importance in the life of the monk and of the monastic family, yet it must be admitted that there is currently much greater emphasis upon the role of the community itself in this regard. Fr. Louis admits this point, even to the extent of admitting that the community might fulfill the role of discernment.

> In Asian traditions as well as in Christian monasticism, there has been considerable stress on the need for a guide or Spiritual Father, an experienced elder who knows how to bring the less experienced to a decisive point of breakthrough where this "new being" is attained. Strictly speaking, Christian monasticism is less dependent on the aid of a guide than some of the other traditions. In Sufism and Zen the spiritual master is as essential as the analyst in psycho-analysis. In Christian monasticism, a fervent community, a living and "spiritual" (pneumatikos) celebration of the liturgical mysteries and of the office, might compensate, to some extent, for the lack of an experienced and charismatic Teacher. (*"Final Integration,"* pp. 2–3)

In Christian monasticism of the cenobitic tradition, the community is so important that he can write: "the essential of our life is not precisely or chiefly that it disposes us for contemplation in the sense that I have just described, but that it produced *a community in which the Spirit can speak to us all in different ways*" (*ibid.*).

This means that renewal cannot be decided merely by each

one individually, nor can it be imposed upon all uniformly. Renewal will depend largely upon the concrete community and its own situation. The community itself must determine the limitations which will or will not aid in this common search for the heart of reality.

According to this view, the monastic community is in possession not so much of a body of detailed and more or less infallible and rigid principles, governing all the minutiae of one's daily life and worship, and systematizing all one's communal relationships; but rather the Holy Spirit, working through the humility and charity of the brethren in their loving acceptance of their Rule and their Spiritual Father, enables them all to keep the commandments and counsels of Christ within the framework of rather flexible observances and practices which are not regarded as so perfect that they cannot be changed without extraordinary legislation.

Depending less on the support of legislation in black and white, the community puts its trust in the love and grace of Christ. Believing that the Holy Spirit has been granted to the community to be a source of light and life, and acting in a spirit of openness and sincerity, the brothers under their Father seek to work out together actual solutions to their own problems. They may certainly come up with answers that are far from ideal in theory, but it may happen by God's grace that these are the particular answers which bring to all of them a possibility of authentic peace, fruitfulness and growth in Christ. ("Monastic Attitudes," *Cistercian Studies*, 1967, I, 8)

Merton sees this exemplified in Ch. 14 of St. John's Gospel. It is this communal possession of the Spirit, this communal search for the Spirit, that gives meaning to the life that the monk chooses to live and that gives direction to the renewal which the monk is called upon to create. For the frontiers of reality which the monk wishes to pierce are not merely a metaphysical or Platonic realm of Being. Concretely and theologically it is the Spirit Himself.

But this Spirit, as has been seen, speaks to the community members in different ways. Fr. Louis sees that the community will be made up of two main classes of people. St. Bernard referred to these classes in relation to the gospel of Martha and Mary. The monastic life is directed towards self-transcendence, towards final integration, towards passing beyond the frontiers of sensible reality. A man comes to the monastery and submits to this way of life precisely because he wants to achieve this, at least to some degree. This is common to all. But the *way* by which one attains to this will vary from one person to the next. The Spirit leads each in His own way, and it is for the community to authenticate this, but also to accept and further this. One may be led specifically by a way of contemplative prayer. This prayer will not be seen as a lessening of one's contact with the community, even if this prayer might lead one into fuller solitude. On the other hand there will be those (and he admits that these will probably be in the majority) "whose life is centered on a kind of simple active service and worship within the cloister, without a thought of mystical prayer. And this is a very special, very real kind of vocation. It is content with its service within the cloister. It emphatically does not want to become involved in active outside concerns and does want simply to lead a quiet, well-ordered life in the cloister centered principally on liturgical worship, on manual work, simple service, communal life and fraternal charity" ("Is the 'Contemplative Life' Finished?," p. 47).

This type of vocation is a monastic vocation in its own right, and these monks are also called to self-transcendence. Their life not only takes on meaning from the fact that their service enables the others to live a contemplative life, but has a meaning of its own. Its meaning comes from the fact that these monks accept the same basic limitations and the same basic discipline of the monastic life in order that they might attain to the same self-transcendence, the same transformation, the same "experience" of monasticism and of the things of God. The difference lies in the way by which they strive for this. While some monks realize this specifically through their life of prayer in the strict sense of the word, others may realize it through a life of more active service.

The specifically "monastic" quality of the life comes, not so much from the exercise itself that is performed, but rather from the effect that it has upon the monk. If it genuinely leads to self-transcendence, to the deepening of consciousness, to a gradual preoccupation with the radical inner depth of one's religious beliefs, then it is effectively "monastic." And there is nothing which can say *a priori* that one way of life will bring this about better than another. It depends entirely upon the way that God is leading a soul. In practice it will usually entail a mixture of both.

Now it would be a great mistake to oppose these two to each other because in fact the person who is called to be a contemplative in the cloister is going to be greatly helped toward that end by living this simple life of service that we have been talking about. Also those who live this simple life of cloistered service and liturgical prayer with a certain amount of meditation with reading, will come very close to a kind of simple contemplative peace in their hearts which, however, they will experience in a slightly different way. ("Is the 'Contemplative Life' Finished?," p. 48)

There can be no opposition between these two ways. Neither one can tend to minimize the other nor compare the two. Each one must simply respect the other and center his attention on responding to that call which the Spirit places in his own heart. It is this inner dimension that is most essential to the cloistered life, rather than simply certain exterior things which are (or are *not*) done. This leads Fr. Louis to the conclusion that "it is unfortunate that the life should be officially called contemplative, because the use of the term is ambiguous for these people [called to cloistered service] and causes a lot of doubt and confusion. In practice they solve it by saying that liturgy is contemplation, and that he who is zealous about going to choir on time is a 'true contemplative'" (*ibid.*).

In saying this, Fr. Louis is not trying to assert that one should oppose liturgy and contemplation. He is merely trying to emphasize the fact that the monk must be one who shares to some degree in an actual *experience* of self-transcendence and that there is no exterior reality, whether it be liturgy, enclosure, silence, fraternal service, or whatever, that will automatically ensure this element. The one who is called to a life of cloistered service must continually look into his own heart to perceive whether he is simply becoming enmeshed in activity or whether he is truly using it as a way to experience reality in its deeper dimensions. But likewise the one who is called to a life of more direct prayer must search his heart to verify whether he is truly remaining in a spirit of inner poverty before God or whether he is perhaps simply using words while failing to attain to the reality itself, whether in prayer or in anything else. In such a case he admits that it would be better to have some authentic experience of a much lesser value, rather than simply to *talk* about some higher experience.

Better just to smell a flower in the garden or something like that than to have an unauthentic experience of a much higher value. So therefore I would say that it is very important in the contemplative life *not to over-emphasize the contemplation.* It is good to speak of these things; but if we constantly over-emphasize those things to which access is inevitably something quite rare, we overlook the ordinary authentic experiences of everyday life as real things to enjoy, things to be happy about, things to praise God for. But the ordinary realities of everyday life, the faith and love with which we live our normal human lives, provide the foundation on which we build these "higher things." If there is no foundation, then we have nothing at all! (*Ibid.,* p. 24)

Consequently the essential thing of the life is that it is geared to this experience which is deeper than merely the exercise of service or of prayer, either one. This experience is basically that of love. The monk is a man who is called by God to love: to love God, to love man, and to love all creation.

The essential thing in our life is this fact that it is centered on love as sufficient to itself. Love alone is enough, regardless of whether it produces anything. In the so-called contemplative life, love is sufficient to itself. It does of course work, it does of course do things; but in our life the emphasis is on love above everything else, on faith above everything else. Especially on faith above works! The characteristic of our life is that it makes us realize how much we depend directly on God by faith. How much we depend directly upon the mercy of God, how much we depend upon receiving everything directly through Him, and not through the mediation of our own activity. So that while we continue to act, we act in such a way that this consciousness of dependence on God is greater, more continual, more all-embracing and more satisfactory than it is in the active life. This is what we really seek. ("Is the 'Contemplative Life' Finished?," p. 53)

Here we have a concrete expression of what this "self-transcendence" really is. For we see that it is to be identified basically with love—with a love which sees and accepts our dependence upon the mercy of God. This is the true meaning of the faith of the monk. It is a life which is geared to expressing and *experiencing* this basic dependence upon the mercy of God.

We are at the heart of the matter here, and we can see why it is so difficult to define just what renewal is in the monastic movement. It is not something which is determined by any particular exterior practices. It is something which will open the soul more to receiving the mercy of God and the brethren, as we ask when entering the monastery for the first time. This means that renewal cannot be tied down to certain practices. It rather requires a revitalization of the whole life from *within*. This may be helped by certain changes from without. But the purpose of any such changes remains ever the same: to further the experience of God in one's life, to deepen the experience of love.

This means that certain things must be emphasized; but also that certain things must be more open than in the past. In this respect he cites such areas as art, etc., which can help to open the monk to the true values of life. Likewise he considers the question of the monk's relation to the world:

It is not enough to keep the monks strictly enclosed and remote from all external activity—this does not of itself constitute a sign of the eschatalogical kingdom. On the contrary, very often this limitation constitutes a serious impoverishment of the personalities of the monks and at the same time prevents that impoverishment from becoming public! It is of course true that solitude and silence are essential to the monastic way of life and discipline does contribute very much to the ends for which the monastic communities exist. But the fact remains that people are called to the monastic life so that they may grow and be transformed, "reborn" to a new and more complete identity, and to a more profoundly fruitful existence in peace, in wisdom, in creativity, in love. When rigidity and limitation become ends in themselves they no longer favor growth, they stifle it. ("Final Integration," p. 3)

In his last article Fr. Louis wrote that the life of the monk must contain *both* the monastic reality and an openness to the world:

Monastic life will remain relevant to the future, specifically in the next two generations, insofar as monasteries open themselves to dialogue and exchange with the intellectual community. But for this dialogue to be meaningful, the intellectual community must find in the monasteries both a *monastic reality* (people of depth and simplicity who have acquired the values of monasticism by living them) and *openness to social reality of the 20th century*. It is very possible for *one or other* of these to be achieved in our structures. *It is very difficult for both to be achieved together.* The present structures must be changed if *both* are to be realized. The survival of monasticism *demands* that both be realized. ("Notes on the Future of Monasticism," *Monastic Exchange*, I, 12)

Here again we can see why it is so difficult to point out just what the realities of renewal are. They are simply those realities which will help the monastic community to live out its own vocation. This will vary to a great extent from community to community. And this is why the recent Decree on Pluralism within the Order takes on such importance.

Each community must be left free to determine for itself where and how the Spirit is speaking. Likewise each monk must be left free to a certain extent to find where and how the Spirit is speaking to him. This means that renewal cannot wait for something on the community level. Each monk must proceed to further those things which will benefit his own "experience" of monastic life. But this must be done in conjunction with his concrete community.

Fr. Louis speaks clearly of the fact that we cannot wait for communal renewal before we begin to go further into the monastic experience.

> What one needs to do is to start a conversion and a new life oneself, insofar as he can. Thus, for me, for example, my new life and my contribution to a renewal in monasticism begins within myself and in my own daily life. My work for renewal takes place strictly in my own situation here, not as a struggle with the institution from which I am relatively free now as a hermit, but in an effort to renew my life of prayer in a whole new context, with a whole new understanding of what the contemplative life means and demands. Creativity has to begin with me and I cannot sit here wasting time urging the monastic institution to become creative and prophetic. . . . What each one of us has to do and what I have to do is to buckle down and really start investigating new possibilities in our own life; and if new possibilities mean radical changes, all right. Maybe we need radical changes for which we have to struggle and sweat some blood. Above all we must be more attentive to God's way and God's time, and give everything when it is really demanded. But on the other hand, let these be real changes and not just neurotic upheaval. ("Is the 'Contemplative Life' Finished?," p. 8)*

Accordingly we can say that the monk has truly a role to fulfill within the Church of the present day. But this role he can fulfill only if his life is truly a breakthrough to the heart of reality. Only in this way can he have anything to offer to the world. But this breakthrough can come about only

* Since this article was written several of the works cited have been published in Merton's posthumous volume entitled *Contemplation in a World of Action*, especially "Is the Contemplative Life Finished?" and "Notes on the Future of Monasticism."—EDITOR.

through the monastic community, which agrees on ways to seek and to find God, and in seeking and finding Him, to seek and find the heart of the world. For this reason, renewal cannot be reduced to any particular formula which will be valid for all. It is something which must be *discovered* by each individual and each community. But Fr. Louis saw this discovery as being essential to the future of monasticism.

To combine real monastic depth and experience with openness to the living intellectual and cultural forces of our time requires a special charism. A charism is a gift, but one must struggle to deserve and keep it. The most basic and important thing is the monastic calling to prayer and renunciation and inner transformation—what used to be called the "contemplative life." Each one must place this *first* in some way or other, without adopting foolish and unreal—or dishonest—ways of doing it. You cannot give what you do not have. If our monasteries are truly centers of deeply experienced monastic life, those who are most alive in the outside world will spontaneously come to share our silence and discuss with us their own fruitful insights. It is this exchange and participation which I believe to be of decisive importance for monasteries. But it all depends on solitude and prayer. ("Notes on the Future of Monasticism," *Monastic Exchange*, I, 13)

ANNE SAWORD

A NUN'S TRIBUTE

"Fear not, Karl Barth! Trust in the divine mercy. Though you have grown up to become a theologian, Christ remains a child in you. Your books (and mine) matter less than we might think! There is in us a Mozart who will be our salvation."

Thomas Merton died the same day as Karl Barth, on December 10, 1968. Strange that he should have answered Barth's dream of Mozart—the "divine child," the "central wisdom that comes in tune with the divine and cosmic music and is saved by love"—with this epitaph for both Barth and himself! But Barth died at eighty-two and it was by his own choice that his massive *Church Dogmatics* remained unfinished; he no doubt felt satisfied that he had given all that he was able to give. Merton died at the age of fifty-three, still in full and exuberant activity. If his influence on the outside world was past its peak, his own Order was beginning at last to place considerable reliance in him. A good many members of the Order are afflicted with our own Cistercian brand of the uncertainty pervading the religious life, the Church, and the world at large. Things cannot have been easy, for an honest and sensitive man whose position as a spiritual leader exposed him to every wind of thought that blew. What a catastrophe if *he* had defected! But as far as one could see, he rode the storm buoyantly, unshaken in his faith, and the sight was reassuring. Indeed, one's immediate natural reaction to the news of his death was not only a deep sense of loss, but a touch of dismay. That he should have been removed from the scene so suddenly, with a flick of God's finger, just when we had such need of him! No doubt we shall see the point of it someday.

An account of his life will inevitably be little more than a résumé of his autobiography, *The Seven Storey Mountain (Elected Silence)*. He was born at Prades, in the French Pyrenees, in 1915, and always looked upon France as his spiritual homeland. Both parents were artists and, of course, impecunious. His father was a New Zealander with a dash of Welsh to which Thomas attributed (justly, to judge by some of the photographs) his own grin; and his mother was an American who, like many mothers with their first child, expected too much of him. He was later to suggest that perhaps on the natural plane contemplatives are made by strict mothers.

His youth was a series of kaleidoscopic changes: the move to Long Island when he was a year old; his grandparents' comfortable middle-class home at Douglaston when he was six and his mother was dying; Bermuda and erratic schooling; back to his grandparents', where he absorbed a profound suspicion and hatred of Catholicism; then back to France and "the fountains of the intellectual and spiritual life of the world to which I belonged"; the friendly village in Languedoc, where his father occasionally refereed for the football club but "lived through the season"; the hateful Lycée where, at ten years old, he wrote the second and third of his ten unpublished youthful novels; the farm in Auvergne where he had his first real contact with Catholicism; the prep-school in Surrey where he took happily to very conventional religion; the horsey household in Aberdeenshire, and the depths of loneliness when he received a telegram that seemed to indicate that his father was out of his mind; Oakham School; the sophisticated life at his godfather's London flat; his father's saintliness, and the misery of seeing him slowly dying of a tumor on the brain; Strasbourg; his father's death; his emptiness of God and everything else except William Blake; sudden maturing, with a brief shipboard love affair; Douglaston, Germany, school; blood-poisoning and a resentful apathy towards life and death; Rome, Byzantine mosaics in the churches, a dawning comprehension of Christ as King, and a switch from D. H. Lawrence to the Gospels; the feeling of being visited one night by his father, sudden horror at his own spiritual state, tears and intense prayer; America and the gradual loss of interest in religion; a year at Cambridge—rowdiness, Dante, and modern psychology.

A painful interview with his guardian closed this section of Merton's life, and he crossed to America in a mood of self-disgust. From then on the kaleidoscope was a more interior one, with fewer major changes of scene but even more of mood and thought: Columbia University, a one-meeting membership of the Young Communist League, and student magazines; health foods, and Gilson on God's aseity; a B.A., a master's thesis on Blake, and the desire to live in the presence of God; Bramachari, the imperturbably innocent little monk who gave him a lasting respect for Hindu monasticism and told him to read St. Augustine and *The Imitation of Christ*; Maritain's *Art and Scholasticism*; the urge to go to Mass for the first time, and the urge that drove him out, deeply happy, at the end of the Mass of the Catechumens; reading Joyce for the sake of his portrait of Catholicism; reading Hopkins writing to Newman about becoming a Catholic; the sudden walk to a presbytery to ask for instructions; conditional baptism, November 16, 1938, after a night of anxiety and only six weeks of instruction; back into months of spiritual sluggishness; the sudden decision to become a priest; daily Communion and happiness; Cuba—soaking himself in Catholicism; sudden panic—no vocation to the Franciscans; teaching English at their college; Easter retreat at Gethsemani; Friendship House in Harlem; doubts and hesitations, and finally, Gethsemani: "What I needed was the solitude to expand in breadth and depth and to be simplified out under the gaze of God more or less the way a plant spreads out its leaves in the sun."

The Gethsemani that took in Brother Louis (as he was to become) on December 10, 1941, was already "crowded with postulants and novices." On the day he made his simple profession the names of those chosen for Gethsemani's first foundation were read out in chapter. By the time *The Seven Storey Mountain* had made him well known, two more foundations had been made and another was being planned. It was not, therefore, Merton's books that caused the sudden rush to the American monasteries, though they undoubtedly did much to increase it. He was set to translating and writing from the very beginning of his monastic career, and complained with real anxiety about "this writer who had followed me into the cloister," who "stands and meets me in the doorway of all my prayers, and follows me into church." But one cannot help wondering, with the Irish monk in the answers to our Order's 1966 questionnaire, "what would have happened to Thomas Merton if he had been bottled-up like the rest of us." Anyway, he was not the first Cistercian to have left behind him in the world everything but the art of writing well.

His books are very diversified: verse, autobiography, journals, biographies of saintly Cistercians, monastic history and the monastic life, mystical theology, studies of the Psalms and of the Desert Fathers, and essays on Oriental religions and on contemporary problems such as war and racial injustice. His work was in demand from all quarters—"people are now convinced that I secrete articles like perspiration"—but the publications of his own Order never had to complain of any lack of generosity, or even—notwithstanding his huge correspondence—of promptitude in answering letters. True, he discouraged the idea of a Cistercian magazine in English: "it would probably turn into a rather cheap sheet full of news bulletins to seduce rich benefactors." But he added: "Perhaps in ten years from now the outlook might be better." And just ten years later he was in fact giving valuable help in setting up *Cistercian Studies.* Only one issue of it, up to his death, contained nothing by him, and there were also his reviews in the *Bulletin,* signed, "L.M."

The problems of monasticism were one of the chief subjects that preoccupied him. If the American monasteries, not surprisingly, were unprepared for their flood of vocations and for the religious and social mutations that were soon to put them to the test, that was not Merton's fault. From the beginning down to his article on "Renewal in Monastic Education" in *Cistercian Studies* he was conscious of the need for careful selection and formation. Some of his wisest and most trenchant remarks come in an article in *Monastic Studies* No. 4 on "Monastic Vocation and Modern Thought," where he tries to help those who "are more seriously concerned with not keeping the talent of identity and personal being buried in the routines of a trivial and forfeited existence." He reaches the conclusion that the only answer is life itself, and that "it is our habit of treating everything as a question—in other words of always tugging at things for an 'answer' instead of letting them be themselves—that quite often provokes a vocation crisis in the monastery"; but it is, in fact, a *conclusion*—the end of a serious study—not a facile evasion. That word "tugging," incidentally, illustrates his graphic power: it suggests a puppy, and leaves in the back of the mind the implication that the habit he refers to belongs to the puppy stage of the monastic life. Merton's work was sometimes hasty, and therefore repetitious and syntactically careless, but it was never flabby. He chose the right words and delivered them with punch.

Another preoccupation, as might be expected of a Cistercian writer with a history as turbulent as his, was the prodigal soul's journey back from the *regio dissimilitudinis* to likeness to God. Hidden beneath the empirical self (alienated in the land of unlikeness) he distinguished (following Ruysbroek) a natural image of God, the freedom and intellectuality of the rational animal, immortal, and one in all men; and a supernatural image of God. The natural unity (Zaehner would make a distinction here) can occasionally become an object of consciousness, either spontaneously (Buber) or by the use of ascetical techniques, but this consciousness does little to make us virtuous or reduce our exile from God. The supernatural image of God is possessed by all the baptized, and some of them live according to it; but again, few experience awareness of it. To do so requires the destruction of the empirical self by asceticism, and the baptism of the natural image and its union with the Spirit—the purgative and unitive ways. Christ is the Key of David, who alone, by his grace, can penetrate into these depths of our being; and at the same time, when we have found our true self we have found our identity with Christ and therefore our likeness to the Father. These are themes Professor Zaehner has been working on, though with Teilhardian prolongations, and with a lukewarm attitude to Zen that was unacceptable to Merton. One wishes that they had put their heads together and made things easier for the rest of us by coming to terms at least over terminology. But we must content ourselves with Zaehner's statement that Merton was "the most remarkable mystic of our times" (*The Catholic Church and World Religions*, p. 18).

If Merton was hardly a Teilhardian, he was nevertheless very much concerned by the world's crucial issues. On this point it will be best to quote (with the kind permission of the editor) from Fr. Illtud Evans's article "Elected Speech," in *The Tablet*, November 12, 1966:

> It is this increasing openness to the world that has marked Thomas Merton's writing in recent years—years which, ironically enough, have seen him turn more and more to the eremitical solitude which he has always considered the ideal of the monastic life. His identification with so many movements of social protest—against war, racial injustice and the persecution of minorities of every sort— might at first seem inconsistent with a monk's withdrawal from the field of temporal action. But it is precisely this sense of the contemplative's being *more* concerned with the world than anyone else—but at the ultimate level of his own closeness to God—that gives Thomas Merton's witness its unique importance: "The monk retains his own perspective and his own horizons, which are those of the desert and of exile. But this in itself should enable him to have a special understanding of his fellow man in an age of alienation."

> The alienation is so deep and its effects so devastating that nothing less than a radical understanding can serve to heal the wounds. . . . No-one is more sensitive to the

troubled moral and social climate of America today than is
Fr. Merton. But what he has to say is much more than a
moralizing intervention from outside. His recent writing
. . . reflects the ever-widening range of his interests and of
his compassion. Above all his purpose is to understand, to
discern the signs that a Christian must want to interpret
and relate to a truth that does not alter. . . . He is aware,
certainly, of the actual problems of a real world. . . . But
all the time he is in effect saying that the ground of ultimate hope is not, and never can be, *here*. To say it is here-
after has often in the past meant a withdrawal that is an
abdication of responsibility, a refusal of love. But the
monk is necessarily "a sign of the world to come because
his true perspectives are those of the eschatological Kingdom of God." He shares in the crisis and tragedy of the
world, and perhaps he is their best interpreter because he,
of all men, should know their origin and their outcome.
. . . For the Church in America he has been a providential
sign, embodying in himself a compassion, an awareness of
responsibilities that stretch far beyond the boundaries of
credal allegiance and inherited piety.

Fr. Evans emphasizes the evolution of Merton's thought:
"the confident antitheses, the reliance on established structures with which to confront a crazy world, are gone for
ever." Merton himself was aware of continually changing and
learning. When the French edition of *The Ascent to Truth*
appeared, he prefaced it with a warning that were he then to
treat of the same subject he would probably do so very
differently. He would complete the psychological aspects by a
discussion of the unconscious (evidently he had by then
recovered from some of the aversion to modern psychology
that had resulted from his Cambridge excesses with it), and
would refer more to Scripture and the Fathers and less to
scholasticism: "En un mot, le livre serait très différent de ce
qu'il est." And yet the French edition appeared only seven
years after the English from which it was translated. The evolution in his thought has its amusing side. When he protests
against "certain conceptions of monasticism which seem to
me to be simply a fancy-dress adaptation of what we are

claiming to have renounced," and instances "those pictures of
'the Trappist' with his cowl over his head and his back to the
camera, looking at a lake," one does feel inclined to raise an
eyebrow. No doubt he would willingly have beaten his breast
and laughed.

His mind changed because it was intensely alive and therefore in constant development. But the changes were often
more than merely intellectual. The experience recorded on
pp. 141–42 of *Conjectures of a Guilty Bystander* begins as
an intellectual realization: "though 'out of the world' we are
in the same world as everybody else." Then it becomes a psychological relief: "Thank God, thank God that I *am* like
other men. . . . To think that for sixteen or seventeen years
I have been taking seriously this pure illusion that is implicit
in so much of our monastic thinking." And finally, with the
realization that God himself gloried in becoming a member
of the human race, it becomes, apparently, a mystical experience. He is in the Louisville shopping center and "there is no
way of telling people that they are all walking around shining
like the sun."

It is not surprising that this constant development of so
naturally gifted a personality should have led him out of the
fraterna acies. After four years as Master of Students and ten
as Master of Novices he was at last allowed, in 1965, to retire
to a hermitage in the monastery woods. He had said of the
experience described above: "It is the function of solitude to
make one realize such things with a clarity that would be impossible to anyone completely immersed in . . . all the au-
tomatisms of a tightly collective existence." And undoubtedly
there was this spiritual side to his move into solitude. But it
must be admitted that he was a hermit *sui generis*, who took
a briefcase up to the monastery every day to collect his mail.
I owe to the kindness of Père Charles Dumont the other doc-
uments quoted here, but I can make one contribution of my
own to Mertoniana. I wrote to Fr. Louis in the autumn of
1967 on business connected with the *Bulletin of Monastic
Spirituality*, took the opportunity of thanking him for the
part his books had played in my own vocation, and made

some allusion to his eremitical life. Here is the relevant part of his answer:

> Actually I find the solitary life very happy because it seems to be that for which I was intended. Not that I am a rigorous hermit type: or that I fly from the face of human beings. But it just seems that even when I am alone I cannot find time to fit in all that I want to get done in a day. Twenty four hours are not enough. I do know that the best way to really waste time is to get with a lot of other people: then it will be killed for certain.

This may not be the loftiest spirituality, but—besides being sound common sense, and devotion to his God-given vocation as a writer—it does show his refusal to pose, to play the *grand spirituel*. I have no idea what his preaching was like; but I feel confident that it was not sonorous.

Leaving his hermitage to make a tour of Oriental monasticism would no doubt have marked the beginning of a fresh stage in his spiritual itinerary. He is described as starting off, in October, "absolutely bouncing with expectation."

On December 5, in a postcard from Singapore, he wrote: "My Asian trip has so far been really remarkable. Very fine contacts with Tibetan Buddhists—a good visit to Ceylon and to hermits living in caves there. I do not promise anything on Bangkok—but if I find it worth while I may be able to write. I go there tomorrow. Then to Rawa Seneng [Java] where I will be until the end of the year."

Sr. Mary Bernard Saïd, O.S.B., of the Abbaye Ste-Gertrude, Louvain, was present at the Congress in Bangkok. She writes:

> In the morning [of December 10] he had given his scheduled talk to the monastic superiors of Asia, met together at Bangkok for the purpose of exchanging views on the adaptation of monasticism to the needs of the Asian peoples. The subject of his talk, "Marxism and Monastic Perspectives," was a critical appraisal of Marxist theory and monastic *theoria*. He showed that though Marxism and monasticism are both in their way revolutionary, they have entirely different approaches. Marxism has its own escha-

tological tendencies and may seem at times prophetic, but —and here is Thomas Merton's existential message—, the monk also has a "prophetic" role which depends on his being primarily and entirely a man of God, a man who has surrendered by his vow of *conversatio morum* to the action of the Holy Spirit, the Spirit of the Risen Christ.

Thomas Merton died on the twenty-seventh anniversary of his entering Gethsemani.

A letter written from Gethsemani on December 13 says: "He no doubt had some premonition of his death and everything was ready in his papers etc. . . . His grave is ready on the slope facing west outside the church, under a cedar tree."

Judging from his abbot's homily, he did have some premonition of his death. Certainly, *Conjectures of a Guilty Bystander* deals several times with the subject of death. There is, for example, a beautiful passage on p. 213, on death as a fulfillment when life is freely and gladly surrendered back into the hands of the Creator and Redeemer. But the words that strike the reader most, now, are on p. 171: "I think sometimes that I may soon die though I am not yet old (forty-seven). . . . I have a habitual awareness that I may die, and that, if this is God's will, then I am glad. 'Go ye forth to meet Him.'"

Thérèse Lentfoehr

TWO POEMS

THE FIREBIRD

(*For a monk in winter*)

You said you carried a bird
of fire under your heart
that sang in all weathers so
that you stepped in madrigal,
each swift sandal-print brimmed with
music. But that was in spring
when your trees stood greenly tranced
in pointilliste, and I (careful for you as a sister)
wondered what would happen in
winter when you cave with Juan
de la Cruz, faring leanly
on sparse manna and a cup
of dark torrent?

These days are
come as flying a synapse
of sky your late letter flails
with the storm and drops like snow
to my hand. Breathless, I take
the page to my window to
peer through the slim spokes of words
for a glimpse of your cageling,
touch one lustrous feather, and
make my dark moor shine with its
'Shelley plain.'

                    But only the
north wind moves and sings; when
suddenly, remembering
the light on your face, I stand
small and abashed at my in-
comprehending—for here is
that ingle of quiet where
the intellect unhoods to
that Sun whose alembic sifts
firebird like fountains that
have now (how wonderfully)
become in you a silence—
for the silence is the bird.

OUT OF A CLOUD

(*In Memory of Thomas Merton*)

Sagittarius spells the first year
of our diminishment
remembering an acre of crosses,
new-turned Kentucky clay
and out of an invisible cloud
the small white hail in a shower—

the last giveaway of his secret
who sat with God in a cloud
and told how it was to be startled
into love. Whether he waded
up the oak-shelved path mixing Stravinsky
and plainsong, or sang with

the Beatles in the cabin on the hill
it did not trouble the cloud.
Paradox of monk who from a hermitage
of a thousand windows
watched our world (loving it) and chose it
his *ashram*. At the sign

of the Lotus he flew oceans
to orient mountains
and there came barefoot to the Burning Bush.
The myth of his cloud
was fire. And home over the shouting
Pacific a gentle sky

had him—a silent guest in the belly
of the jet with his much-
mourned Vietnam brothers (each in his gray
catacomb). In this *now* day
of resurrection, these with him we
celebrate, praising

the Creator who in so brief and
desperate a season
shaped us a friend who reached into our
solitudes and with
the finger of a word touched in us the deep
places of the living God.

ECUMENICAL MONK

Thomas Merton's spirit of ecumenism was a natural consequence of his monastic and contemplative experience. In
discussing "Ecumenism and Renewal," he pointed out two
important lines of development, which he felt must intersect
in monasticism: "one, the lived theology which is the monastic experience, and, two, the expansion and opening of perspectives which lead to a lived unity, the common sharing of
Christian grace in crisis, irrespective of Church divisions." He
then added a third line: "the common religious aspirations of
humankind and its groping for transcendent experience, however you may want to qualify it (mystical, prophetic, contemplative, metaphysical, etc.)."

Merton felt keenly that the ecumenical opening of the
monastery "must mean more than just admitting Baptist or
Methodist seminarians to view a living diorama in Church
history. Nor will it be enough for monks who still meditate
(a few do) to get together and compare notes (or swap
mondo) with a Zen *roshi*." In a word, if the monastic life is
to be validly renewed, it must retain or recover a threefold
relevance: first, the monastic life must have an authentic relevance in its own right as a focus of Christian experience with
a monastic orientation, resulting in a "vision" or "contemplation," prophetic and eschatological awareness. Second, the
monastic life must preserve or acquire an ecumenical relevance, in the form of an openness which is not only ready
and able to discuss creedal or sectarian differences with a certain detachment, but which is able to share on the deepest
level the risks and agonies of Christian crises—more than a

sharing of gripes about the stupidities of one's ecclesiastical establishment. Third, the monastic life must prove itself able to be relevant even to the unbeliever who is nevertheless concerned with a self-transcending experience, the unpredictable and unexplained illumination that flashes out of the ground of one's own being. (For a complete treatment of this subject see "Ecumenism and Renewal" in *Contemplation in a World of Action*, pp. 181ff.)

Later in the same article Merton sounds a warning about the wrong kind of concern for relevance with which some monks unfortunately are too much preoccupied: "There are some monks who are so diffident about their charism that they try to make their lives relevant to the rest of the world by systematically emptying them of everything monastic; that is to say, by repudiating all that is eschatological, contemplative, otherworldly, everything that has to do with the desert, with asceticism, with hope and with prayer" (p. 202). He then goes on to stress the need for a dialectic between eschatology and incarnation: "the monk not only retains the eschatological privilege and duty of smashing idols—worldly, ecclesiastical, secular and even monastic—but he also has the incarnational privilege and duty of having his feet on God's ground and his hands in the fruitful dirt."

Merton saw clearly the unique dimension that the monastic life could contribute to ecumenical experience by deepening the unity that comes about not only by dialogue with our separated brethren, but above all by being silent with them, and sharing our solitude with them. A contemplative monastery should provide this kind of atmosphere or climate for mutual fraternal exchange and prayer. "The monastic life (when it is true to its own charism) is pervaded with the sense of the definitive that comes to those who, in silence, refrain from the futility of articulation. Yet also what must be grasped are the provisional needs to be articulated in honest and undogmatic speech. The two go together. The monastic dialectic of silence and language underlines the deeper dialectic of eschatology and incarnation" (p. 210). In this, Merton the monk was a real master, according to the testimony of those who had the good fortune to enter into conversation with him on a deep level.

As a pioneer in ecumenical encounter, Thomas Merton inaugurated contacts with innumerable groups of both Christians and non-Christians long before ecumenism had gained momentum and had become a respectable movement within the Christian churches. These informal efforts began in the fifties when groups of Baptists, Methodists, Disciples of Christ, and Episcopalians from nearby Kentucky, Indiana, and Tennessee seminaries or exchange students from various Midwestern universities would spend a day or two at the Abbey of Gethsemani, attend the liturgical offices and Eucharistic celebration with the monks, and then enter into ecumenical discussions with Father Merton and a group of his confreres.

At other times it might be the solitary visit of a non-Christian of the stature of Rabbi Abraham Heschel or an Oriental student who had come to the monastery in search of the ultimate meaning in life. To all Merton gave of himself wholeheartedly, and at the same time, as he frankly admitted, he learned very much from these contacts. His whole background and education eminently qualified him for this kind of encounter with men of different religious beliefs. He considered such dialogue a natural overflow of his own monastic experience.

But Merton's true ecumenical spirit cannot adequately be seen until it is viewed in the context of his enormous correspondence and journals, as well as his increasingly diversified writings in the fifties and sixties. In a beautiful passage from one of his journals, *Conjectures of a Guilty Bystander*, he writes of the spirit of ecumenism that welled up within him:

> If I can unite *in myself* the thought and the devotion of Eastern and Western Christendom, the Greek and the Latin Fathers, the Russians with the Spanish mystics, I can prepare in myself the reunion of divided Christians. From that secret and unspoken unity in myself can eventually come a visible and manifest unity of all Christians. If we want to bring together what is divided, we cannot do so

by imposing one division upon the other or absorbing one division into the other. But if we do this, the union is not Christian. It is political, and doomed to further conflict. We must contain all divided worlds in ourselves and transcend them in Christ. (p. 12)

After spending a day with a group of Asian, African, and European journalists studying at Indiana University, discussing religious problems of modern man, Merton related to his fellow monks what a tremendously rewarding experience this was for him. Like St. Paul, he was convinced that he must "become all things to all men"—that he must become a "universal man" in the sense of sharing in some measure the lot of the Jew, the Hindu, the Buddhist, the Muslim. He felt especially attracted to Sufism, and spoke often to his community of Sufi poetry and mysticism, although he concentrated on Zen Buddhism in his later writings. "If I understand something of how a Muslim looks at God, the unity of God, it is going to increase my appreciation of the Christian dogma of the unity of God," he confessed to a group of monks afterwards. Their hunger and thirst for Truth is somewhat different from that of a Christian, and only by entering into this experience could he become a universal, catholic Christian.

This same universality of interest and concern can be seen in a sampling of his correspondence published in *Seeds of Destruction*. In a letter to the Shaker authority, Edward Deming Andrews, for whom Merton had written an introduction to his book on Shaker furniture, he wrote: "The Shakers remain as witnesses to the fact that only humility keeps a man in communion with truth, and first of all with his own inner truth. This one must know without knowing it, as they did. For as soon as a man becomes too self-consciously aware of his truth, he lets go of it and embraces an illusion" (p. 260).

Merton often visited the Shaker village at Pleasant Hill, Kentucky, on his frequent trips to Lexington to visit the doctor. He photographed the old buildings (later restored) on one occasion and wrote an enthusiastic article, which was subsequently published in *Mystics and Zen Masters*. He admired their wonderful simplicity of life and regretted their disappearance: "After their departure, these innocent people, who had once been so maligned, came to be regretted, loved and idealized. Too late the people of Kentucky recognized the extraordinary importance of the spiritual phenomenon that had blossomed out in their midst" (p. 201).

Writing to a Rabbi friend, he asked for more information about the Kibbutz, and then went on to comment on the fact that the Jews are the great eschatalogical sign of the twentieth century:

> Everything comes to depend on people understanding this fact, not just reacting to it with a little appropriate feeling, but seeing the whole thing as a sign from God, telling. Telling us what? Among other things, telling Christians that if they don't look out they are going to miss the boat or fall out of it, because the antinomy they have unconsciously and complacently supposed between the Jews and Christ is not even a good figment of the imagination. The suffering Servant is One, Christ, Israel. There is one wedding and one wedding feast, not two or five or six. There is one bride. There is one mystery, and the mystery of Israel and of the Church is ultimately to be revealed as One. (p. 273)

Of all Merton's books, perhaps *Conjectures of a Guilty Bystander* is the most ecumenical in character. Yet, he declares in the preface that it is not "a professional book of ecumenism." Rather his approach is completely personal and informal. He simply records ways in which theologians like Barth and Bonhoeffer have entered quite naturally and easily into his personal, monastic, and Christian world-view. The book demonstrates admirably how a contemplative monk could read Barth and Bonhoeffer and identify with them in much the same way as he could with Catholic writers like Maritain and Gilson. Merton maintained that the book was "a Catholic sharing the Protestant experience, and other religious experiences as well." This does not mean that he agreed completely with Barth, Bonhoeffer, or Robinson, but he confessed, nevertheless: "Some of their books have proved relevant and stimulating to me in a cloistered and contemplative monastery. In the climate of Second Vatican Council, this no longer requires apology or justification." Merton concludes his preface with these astute reflections on the role of the monk in an age of ecumenicism: "If the Catholic Church is turning to the modern world and to the other Christian Churches, and if she is perhaps for the first time seriously taking note of non-Christian religions in their own terms, then it becomes necessary for at least a few contemplative and monastic theologians to contribute something of their own to the discussion. . . . The singular, existential, poetic approach is proper to this monastic view" (p. vii).

The first journal entry records Barth's dream about Mozart, which moved Merton deeply. In his dream about Mozart, Barth remarks that it is a "child, even a divine child that speaks to us in Mozart's music." Yet Mozart refused to answer the theologian's questions. Merton comments on this: "Fear not, Karl Barth! Trust in the divine mercy. Though you have grown up to become a theologian, Christ remains a child in you. Your books (and mine) matter less than we might think! There is in us a Mozart who will be our salvation." Coincidentally, Karl Barth and Thomas Merton died on the same day, December 10, 1968, and shared an obituary on the front page of the *New York Times*. On the day of Merton's funeral at Gethsemani, a Barth-Merton ecumenical memorial service was held in Louisville, where Catholics, Protestants, Hindus, and Jews all paid their respects to these two great religious men of our day, so different and yet so similar in many respects. As Father Eugene Zoeller remarked in the homily at this Memorial Mass: "I think we would be making a serious mistake if we linked these two great men together only by the sheer coincidence of death. That which united them radically and inseparably was life, *life itself*; for each, life was and remains the insatiable quest for God and Him that he has sent, Jesus Christ. Together in quest, together in hope, and now, together in the eternal discovery of God" (unpublished manuscript).

In the early sixties Merton's attention became more focused on the East and its various religious and philosophical disciplines. In writing to a Chinese priest in California he had this to say, which may shock those of a strictly Catholic ghetto mentality who feel they have nothing to receive from the Asian traditions:

> I do not know if I have anything to offer Asians, but I am convinced that I have an immense amount to learn from Asia. One of the things I would like to share with Asians is not only Christ, but Asia itself. I am convinced that a rather superficial Christianity in European dress is not enough for Asia. We have lacked depth. We have lacked the breadth of view to grasp all the wonderful breadth and richness in the Asian traditions, which were given to China, India, Japan, Korea, Burma, etc., as natural preparations for the coming of Christ. (p. 283)

He went on to say that he felt that those who finally brought Christ had fallen short of the preparation that the Holy Spirit had provided, and that the problem was increased by the fact that Asians had renounced Asia to a great extent, and tried desperately to imitate the West.

The exchange of correspondence between Merton and Suzuki continued over a number of years and culminated in a meeting between them on Dr. Suzuki's last visit to America. Merton referred to this meeting later in an article "Learning How to Live" published in *University on the Heights* by Columbia University Press, which makes evident the communication that was achieved on the deepest level between these two men of totally different traditions. Their correspondence was later published in *Zen and the Birds of Appetite*. This volume, dedicated to his friend, Amiya Chakravarty, for whom he had the greatest affection, is another example of Merton's boundless ecumenical spirit. He believed firmly that Christianity and Zen "can complement each other, and for this reason Zen is perfectly compatible with Christian belief and indeed with Christian mysticism (if we understand Zen in its pure state, as metaphysical intuition)" (p. 47).

Thomas Merton's *Asian Journal* makes clear his great love

for Asia and the real basis of his interest in Zen. In a fascinating letter from Asia shortly after his three visits to the Dalai Lama, published as an appendix to that volume, Merton does not conceal his admiration for the Dalai Lama and expresses their profound agreement. It was not a case of abandoning his Christian commitment, as some had believed, but rather his pilgrimage to the East was seen as a way of deepening his own contemplative experience. This is quite evident from the prepared remarks for an interfaith meeting held in Calcutta in mid-November of 1968, scarcely three weeks before his death in Bangkok, Thailand:

> I speak as a Western monk who is pre-eminently concerned with his own monastic calling and dedication. I have left my monastery to come here not just as a research scholar or even as an author (which I happen to be). I come as a pilgrim who is anxious not just to obtain information, not just facts about other monastic traditions, but to drink from ancient sources of monastic vision and experience. I seek not only to learn more (quantitatively) about religion and monastic life, but to become a better and more enlightened monk (qualitatively) myself. (*Asian Journal of Thomas Merton*, Appendix)

In addressing the Asian monastic leaders at Bangkok a few weeks later on the subject of Marxism and monastic perspectives, Merton concluded his remarks with a frank appreciation of the monastic values of the East as a complement to our Western Christian monasticism: "I believe that by openness to Buddhism, to Hinduism, and to these great Asian traditions, we stand a wonderful chance of learning more about the potentiality of our own traditions. . . . The combination of the natural techniques and the graces and the other things that have been manifested in Asia, and the Christian liberty of the Gospel should bring us all at last to that full and transcendent liberty which is beyond mere cultural differences and mere externals . . ." (*ibid.*).

This was Thomas Merton's last ecumenical statement to the world, and it was uttered in all seriousness only two hours before his accidental death in a small Bangkok cottage room.

Never in my life have I known a man more dedicated to his own monastic vocation of Christian witness, and at the same time completely open to the Spirit in whatever way it might be made manifest. May the Lord in His mercy raise up in our day more men of his vision and dedication to the Gospel message: "that they all may be one."

EPILOGUE: A HOMILY

My dear Fathers and Brothers,

Last week we buried one of our older brothers, Brother Leo, a serious man who lived a long and silent life for the Lord. Today we celebrate this Mass on the occasion of another Brother's passing to the Lord, our own Father Louis.

This was a younger Brother, even a boyish Brother, one who could have lived a hundred years without growing old.

His life was far from silent, despite his hermit bent, since he was, in God's Providence, an artful minister of the Word. The world knew him from his books, we knew him from his spoken word. Few, if any, knew him in his secret prayer.

Still, he had a secret prayer and this is what gave the inner life to all he said and wrote. His secret was his secret to himself to a great extent, but he was a skillful reader of the secret of the souls that sought his help. It was because of this that although we laughed at him, and with him, as we would a younger Brother, still we respected him as the spiritual father of our souls.

Those of us who had the privilege and pleasure to deal with Father Louis on intimate terms, and submit our inner lives to his direction, know that in him we had the best of Spiritual Fathers.

He was, then, both a Brother and a Father, and to those who wished it, he was also a faithful friend. To me, personally, he was one of the most helpful and lovable men that I have ever had the pleasure to meet. I owe him more than words can say. His passing is a great loss. However, we know that it is not a complete loss. He has left his mark deep in this community, and it will be with us for years to come, for he has planted it in the hearts of a generation, and God willing, it will be planted again for generations to come.

Each of you, I am sure, would read his message somewhat differently and this, of course, is the way he would have it. But the message is basically the same for all. We are men of God only insofar as we are seeking God, and God will only be found by us insofar as we find Him in the truth about ourselves. Silence, solitude, and seclusion are means to this and nothing more. The end of all is purity of faith and love, and the thing that keeps us going is our hope.

Father Louis undertook this trip to Asia in the spirit of this same quest for God. His letters to me from there were buoyant with hope for further progress in his quest.

The possibility of death was not absent from his mind. We spoke of this before he set out—first jokingly, then seriously. He was ready for it. He even saw a certain fittingness in dying over there amidst those Asian monks, who symbolized for him man's ancient and perennial desire for the deep things of God.

Therefore, although he has died away from us in body, he did not die away from us in spirit. His death may be painful for us, but it is joy for him, for it is the fulfilling at long last of the quest for God and the hope in God which was his.

May God reward him then for all that he has done for this community, and may the quest for God, and hope in God, which was his, remain on now in us, that we too may share with him some day the joy of fulfillment in the Kingdom of our Father.

This we ask through Christ Our Lord and through the intercession of His holy Mother. Amen.

NOTES ON THE CONTRIBUTORS

Abbot John Eudes Bamberger, O.C.S.O., entered the Cistercian Abbey of Gethsemani in 1950 as an M.D. After profession and ordination he studied psychiatry in Washington, D.C., and theology in Rome. In 1969 he was chosen
Secretary General of the *Concilium Generale* and in 1971
he was elected Abbot of the monastery of the Genesee
near Rochester, New York, a foundation from Gethsemani.

Abbot Flavian Burns, O.C.S.O., has been a monk of Gethsemani since 1951. After his ordination to the priesthood
he was sent to Rome to study Canon Law at the Gregorian
University. After Abbot James Fox's resignation in 1968,
he was elected Abbot by the community at Gethsemani.
He retired in 1973 and is presently living in a small hermitage at Gethsemani. Abbot Flavian was superior at the
time of Father Merton's death, and preached the homily
published here the day following his death.

Father Aldhelm Cameron-Brown, O.S.B., a Benedictine
monk of Prinknash Abbey in Gloucester, England, entered
the Catholic Church while a student at Cambridge in
1952, inspired by his reading of Thomas Merton. In 1970
he came to America to attend the Cistercian Symposium
in Georgia, and at the same time visited Gethsemani and
the Merton hermitage.

Father Tarcisius Conner, O.C.S.O., a monk of Gethsemani,
is currently located at Christ in the Desert Monastery at
Abiquiu, New Mexico. After his ordination to the priesthood, he continued his theological studies at the Gregorian
University in Rome, where he earned his S.T.L. Since his
return to Gethsemani he has taught theology and contrib-
utes regularly to monastic and literary journals.

Father Charles Dumont, O.C.S.O., is a Cistercian monk at
the Abbey of Scourmont in Belgium, where he entered in
1941. After his ordination in 1950 he spent ten years at
the Cistercian Abbey on Caldey Island in Wales. A correspondent with Father Merton for fifteen years, he was able
to meet him in his hermitage at Gethsemani in January,

1968. Father Dumont has been chief editor of the review *Collectanea Cisterciensia* since 1962.

Abbot James Fox, O.C.S.O., a native of Boston, was educated at Harvard University before entering the Abbey of Gethsemani in 1927. He was first superior at the foundation of Holy Spirit monastery in Conyers, Georgia, and was elected its first abbot in 1946. Upon the death of Abbot Frederic Dunne in 1948, he was elected Abbot of Gethsemani and remained so until his resignation in January of 1968. Since that time he has been living as a hermit on Gethsemani's property a few miles south of the monastery.

Brother Patrick Hart, O.C.S.O., was educated at the University of Notre Dame, and after a brief teaching career, entered Gethsemani in 1951. He served as secretary to Abbot James Fox for ten years prior to his assignment to the General's House in Rome. Upon his return he became Merton's secretary. At present he is the Abbey's representative on Merton affairs, and edited the present volume.

Father Matthew Kelty, O.C.S.O., has been a monk of Gethsemani since 1960. He joined at forty-five, coming from the Society of the Divine Word, a missionary society, and was a novice for two and a half years under Thomas Merton. He now lives as a hermit (still a member of the Gethsemani community) in the mission where he worked twenty-five years ago—New Guinea. For the past three years he was head of an experimental monastery in Oxford, North Carolina.

Father Jean Leclercq, O.S.B., is a Benedictine monk of Clervaux Abbey in Luxembourg. As a monastic scholar and historian he is especially known for his critical edition of the works of St. Bernard. Besides his numerous books and articles in French, he is the author of the following books in English translation: *Love of Learning and the Desire of God* (Fordham University Press), *Alone with God* (Farrar, Straus & Giroux), *The Way of Perfection* (Liturgical Press). An old friend of Father Merton, he corresponded with him from 1950 to 1968.

Sister Thérèse Lentfoehr, S.D.S., a member of the Congregation of the Sisters of the Divine Savior, is "Poet in Residence" at the College of Racine in Wisconsin. She has been an old friend and correspondent with Merton since

1939 and visited him a number of times at Gethsemani. Herself a published poet, she has recently written a critical study on the poetry of Thomas Merton entitled, "Beautiful Cellars."

Brother Patrick Ryan, O.C.S.O., after attending Fordham University, entered the Abbey of the Genesee, Piffard, New York, in 1961. He has published a number of articles on monastic history and spirituality. In September of 1973 he began a course of studies leading to a Master's Degree in Medieval Studies at Western Michigan University, Kalamazoo, Michigan. He is particularly interested in William of St. Thierry and in relating Christian monastic tradition to the spiritual traditions of Africa and Asia.

Sister Anne Saword, O.C.S.O., was born in England and baptized in the Anglican Church. After two years with the Plymouth Brethren, she embraced Catholicism in 1953 and did her university studies in Russian. In 1956 she entered the Cistercian Convent of Stapehill in Dorset. Later she transferred to the Cistercian Convent of Chimay in Belgium, while still remaining a member of Stapehill. Since 1969 she has been co-editor of *Cistercian Studies*, the English-speaking counterpart of *Collectanea Cisterciensia*.

Brother David Steindl-Rast, O.S.B., was born in Vienna, where he studied art, anthropology, and psychology. In 1953 he joined the newly-founded Benedictine monastery of Mount Saviour, Pine City, New York, where he received formal training in philosophy and theology. He has studied and practiced Zen at the Zen Studies Society in New York, and in 1968 Brother David organized a Center for Spiritual Studies in which Buddhists, Hindus, Jews, and Christians participate.

Thirty Poems	Verse	New Directions	1944
A Man in the Divided Sea	Verse	New Directions	1946
Figures for an Apocalypse	Verse	New Directions	1948
The Seven Storey Mountain	Autobiography	Harcourt, Brace	1948
"	* "	Doubleday Image	
Exile Ends in Glory	Biography	Bruce	1948
Seeds of Contemplation	Religion	New Directions	1949
"	* "	Dell	
The Waters of Siloe	History	Harcourt, Brace	1949
"	* "	Doubleday Image	
The Tears of the Blind Lions	Verse	New Directions	1949
What Are These Wounds?	Biography	Bruce	1950
The Ascent to Truth	Theology	Harcourt, Brace	1951
"	* "	Viking Compass	
The Sign of Jonas	Journal	Harcourt, Brace	1953
"	* "	Doubleday Image	
Bread in the Wilderness	Theology	New Directions	1953
"	* "	Liturgical Press	
The Last of the Fathers	Theology	Harcourt, Brace	1954
"	"		
	(reprint)	Greenwood	1970
No Man Is an Island	Religion	Harcourt, Brace	1955
"	* "	Doubleday Image	
The Living Bread	Theology	Farrar, Straus	1956
"	* "	Dell	
Thomas Merton: A Bibliography	Bibliography	Farrar, Straus	1956
The Strange Islands	Verse	New Directions	1956
The Tower of Babel	Verse Play	New Directions	1957

* refers to paperback edition—Editor.

The Silent Life	Religion	Farrar, Straus	1957
"	* "	Dell	
Thoughts in Solitude	Religion	Farrar, Straus	1958
"	* "	Doubleday Image	
The Secular Journal of Thomas Merton	Journal	Farrar, Straus	1959
"	* "	Dell	
Selected Poems	Verse	New Directions	1959
"			
(enlarged edition)	* "	New Directions	
Spiritual Direction and Meditation	Religion	Liturgical Press	1960
The Wisdom of the Desert	Religion	New Directions	1960
Disputed Questions	Essays	Farrar, Straus	1960
"	* "	New American Library	
The Behavior of Titans	Prose poems, essays	New Directions	1961
New Seeds of Contemplation	Religion	New Directions	1961
"	* "	New Directions	1961
The New Man	Theology	Farrar, Straus	1961
"	* "	New American Library	
Original Child Bomb	Prose poem	New Directions	1962
A Thomas Merton Reader	Anthology	Harcourt, Brace	1962
Life and Holiness	Religion	Herder & Herder	1963
"	* "	Doubleday Image	
Emblems of a Season of Fury	*Verse	New Directions	1963
Seeds of Destruction	Essays	Farrar, Straus	1964
"	* "	Macmillan	
The Way of Chuang Tzŭ	Philosophy	New Directions	1965
"	* "	New Directions	
Seasons of Celebration	Religion	Farrar, Straus	1965
Raids on the Unspeakable	*Prose poems	New Directions	1966
Conjectures of a Guilty Bystander	Notes	Doubleday	1966
"	* "	Doubleday Image	
Mystics and Zen Masters	Essays	Farrar, Straus	1967
"	* "	Delta	

Cables to the Ace	Prose poems	New Directions	1968
"	* "	New Directions	
Faith and Violence	*Essays	Notre Dame	1968
Zen and the Birds of Appetite	Essays	New Directions	1968
"	* "	New Directions	
My Argument with the Gestapo	Novel	Doubleday	1969
The Geography of Lograire	Long poem	New Directions	1969
"	* "	New Directions	
The True Solitude	Selected essays	Hallmark	1969
The Climate of Monastic Prayer	Religion	Cistercian Publications	1969
Contemplative Prayer (same as above)	"	Herder & Herder	1969
"	* "	Doubleday Image	
A Hidden Wholeness (John Howard Griffin and Thomas Merton)	Photo Essay	Houghton Mifflin	1970
Contemplation in a World of Action	Essays	Doubleday	1971
"	* "	Doubleday Image	
Thomas Merton on Peace	Essays	McCall	1971
Opening the Bible	Scripture	Liturgical Press	1971
The Asian Journal of Thomas Merton	Journal	New Directions	1973
Thomas Merton: A Bibliography (updated)	Bibliography	Scarecrow Press	1974

TRANSLATIONS:

The Soul of the Apostolate: J. B. Chautard	Introduction by Merton	Gethsemani	1946
"	* "	Doubleday Image	1961

Clement of Alexandria:
Selections from the Pro-
treptikos   *   New Directions 1962
The Solitary Life:
A Letter of Guigo the
Carthusian   *   Stanbrook
                                              Abbey   1963

A Prayer of Cassiodorus:
From *De Anima*
Treatise   *   Stanbrook
                                              Abbey   1967

Also translations of verse by Raissa Maritain, Jorge Carrera
Andrade, Nicanor Parra, Fernando Pessoa, Ernesto Cardenal,
Pablo Antonio Cuadra, Cesar Vallejo, etc. published in New
Directions anthologies. His translations of Rene Char pub-
lished by Unicorn Press, Santa Barbara, 1969.

EDITOR:
Breakthrough to Peace   New Directions 1963
Gandhi on Non-violence   New Directions 1965
Monks Pond (a journal of
poetry)   Gethsemani   1968

SELECTED PAMPHLETS:
Praying the Psalms   Liturgical Press 1956
*Basic Principles of Mo-
nastic Spirituality*   Gethsemani   1957
Monastic Peace   Gethsemani   1958
*Monastic Life at
Gethsemani*   Gethsemani   1966
Gethsemani, Life of Praise   Gethsemani   1966
Albert Camus' The Plague:
Introduction and Com-
mentary   Seabury Press 1968

HAMMER LIMITED EDITIONS:
Prometheus/A Meditation   U. of Ky. King
                                              Lib. Press   1958
What Ought I To Do?   Stamperia del
                                              Santuccio   1959

The Solitary Life	Stamperia del Santuccio	1960
Hagia Sophia	Stamperia del Santuccio	1962
Early Poems/1940–1942	The Anvil Press	1971
Pasternak/Merton: Six Letters	U. of Ky. King Lib. Press	1973

1915   Jan. 31. Born at Prades (Pyr. Or.) France, son of Owen Merton, artist from New Zealand, and Ruth Jenkins, artist from Ohio, U.S.A.

1916   Moved to U.S.A.: Maryland and New York. Lived at Flushing, L.I., and at Douglaston, L.I. (with mother's family).

1921   Death of mother, cancer of stomach, Bellevue Hospital, N.Y.

1922   Went to Bermuda, attended elementary school.

1923   Returned to Douglaston

1925   Went to France with father. Residence at St. Antonin (T. et G.).

1926   Entered Lycée Ingres, Montauban, France.

1928   Went to England.

1929   Entered Oakham School. (Rutland, England).

1931   Death of father, brain tumor, Middlesex Hospital, London (January).

1932   At Oakham, acquired Higher Certificate and Scholarship to Clare College, Cambridge.

1933   Visit to Italy, summer in U.S.A., entered Cambridge in fall. Studied modern languages (French and Italian).

1934   Gained second in Modern Language Tripos Part I, Cambridge. Moved to N.Y.

1935   February. Entered Columbia University.

1937   At Columbia, editor of 1937 *Yearbook*, art editor of Columbia *Jester*.

1938   Graduated from Columbia, B.A. Began work on M.A. Thesis: *Nature and Art in William Blake*.

1939   M.A. Columbia. Teaching in University Extension (English).

1939–1941   Teaching English at St. Bonaventure University (Franciscan Fathers), New York. Contributing to *New York Times Book Review* and *New York Herald Tribune*, as well as to literary magazines.

1941   December 10. Entered Abbey of Gethsemani (Cistercians), Kentucky.

1944 March 19. Simple Vows.
1947 March 19. Solemn Vows.
1949 May 26 (Ascension). Ordained priest at Gethsemani by Archbishop John A. Floersh of Louisville.
1951–1955 Master of the Students (*Magister Spiritus*), Gethsemani.
1955–1965 Master of Novices, Gethsemani.
1963 Awarded Medal for Excellence, Columbia University.
1964 Honorary L.D., University of Kentucky.
1965 Permitted to retire to hermitage.
1968 December 10. Died at Bangkok, Thailand, where he was invited to attend a meeting of Asian Benedictine and Cistercian abbots, monks and nuns.

OTHER IMAGE BOOKS

These prices subject to change without notice

OTHER IMAGE BOOKS

THE LIFE OF TERESA OF JESUS: The Autobiography of St. Teresa of Avila. Trans. and ed. by E. Allison Peers (D96) – $2.45

THE CONFESSIONS OF ST. AUGUSTINE – Translated with an Introduction by John K. Ryan (D101) – $1.75

SPIRITUAL CANTICLE – St. John of the Cross. Trans. and ed. by E. Allison Peers (D110) – $2.95

A WOMAN CLOTHED WITH THE SUN – Edited by John J. Delaney (D118) – $1.75

INTERIOR CASTLE – St. Teresa of Avila (Translated by E. Allison Peers) – (D120) – $1.75

THE GREATEST STORY EVER TOLD – Fulton Oursler (D121) – $1.75

LIVING FLAME OF LOVE – St. John of the Cross (Translated by E. Allison Peers) – (D129) – $1.45

A HISTORY OF PHILOSOPHY: VOLUME 1 – GREECE AND ROME (2 Parts) – Frederick Copleston, S.J. (D134a, D134b) – $1.75 ea.

A HISTORY OF PHILOSOPHY: VOLUME 2 – MEDIAEVAL PHILOSOPHY (2 Parts) – Frederick Copleston, S.J. Part I – Augustine to Bonaventure. Part II – Albert the Great to Duns Scotus (D135a, D135b) – Pt. I, $1.95; Pt. II, $1.75

A HISTORY OF PHILOSOPHY: VOLUME 3 – LATE MEDIAEVAL AND RENAISSANCE PHILOSOPHY (2 Parts) – Frederick Copleston, S.J. Part I – Ockham to the Speculative Mystics. Part II – The Revival of Platonism to Suárez (D136a, D136b) – Pt. I, $1.75; Pt. II, $1.45

A HISTORY OF PHILOSOPHY: VOLUME 4 – MODERN PHILOSOPHY: Descartes to Leibniz – Frederick Copleston, S.J. (D137) – $1.75

A HISTORY OF PHILOSOPHY: VOLUME 5 – MODERN PHILOSOPHY: The British Philosophers, Hobbes to Hume (2 Parts) – Frederick Copleston, S.J. Part I – Hobbes to Paley (D138a) – $1.45. Part II – Berkeley to Hume (D138b) – $1.75

A HISTORY OF PHILOSOPHY: VOLUME 6 – MODERN PHILOSOPHY (2 Parts) – Frederick Copleston, S.J. Part I – The French Enlightenment to Kant (D139a, D139b) – $1.45 ea.

A HISTORY OF PHILOSOPHY: VOLUME 7 – MODERN PHILOSOPHY (2 Parts) – Frederick Copleston, S.J. Part I – Fichte to Hegel. Part II – Schopenhauer to Nietzsche (D140a, D140b) – $1.75 ea.

These prices subject to change without notice

OTHER IMAGE BOOKS

A HISTORY OF PHILOSOPHY: VOLUME 8 – MODERN PHILOSOPHY: Bentham to Russell (2 Parts) – Frederick Copleston, S.J. Part I – British Empiricism and the Idealist Movement in Great Britain. Part II – Idealism in America, the Pragmatist Movement, the Revolt against Idealism (D141a, D141b) – $1.75 ea.

A DOCTOR AT CALVARY – Pierre Barbet, M.D. (D155) – 95¢

THE SPIRITUAL EXERCISES OF ST. IGNATIUS – Translated by Anthony Mottola, Ph.D. Introduction by Robert W. Gleason, S.J. (D170) – $1.45

THE WAY OF PERFECTION – St. Teresa of Avila. Trans. and ed. by E. Allison Peers (D176) – $1.75

LIFE AND HOLINESS – Thomas Merton (D183) – $1.25

MY LIFE WITH CHRIST – Anthony J. Paone, S.J. (D185) – $1.95

A FAMILY ON WHEELS: Further Adventures of the Trapp Family Singers – Maria Augusta Trapp with Ruth T. Murdoch (D187) – $1.25

WITH GOD IN RUSSIA – Walter J. Ciszek, S.J., with Daniel L. Flaherty, S.J. (D200) – $1.95

A HOPKINS READER – Ed. by John Pick (D203) – $2.45

THE TWO-EDGED SWORD – John L. McKenzie, S.J. (D215) – $1.45

THE LILIES OF THE FIELD – William E. Barrett (D225) – 95¢

NO MAN IS AN ISLAND – Thomas Merton (D231) – $1.45

AND YOUNG MEN SHALL SEE VISIONS – Andrew M. Greeley (D232) – 85¢

CONJECTURES OF A GUILTY BYSTANDER – Thomas Merton (D234) – $1.45

THE POWER OF LOVE – Fulton J. Sheen (D235) – $1.25

THE NOONDAY DEVIL: Spiritual Support in Middle Age – Bernard Basset, S.J. (D237) – $1.25

HEALTH OF MIND AND SOUL – Ignace Lepp (D239) – 95¢

RELIGION AND PERSONALITY – Adrian van Kaam, C.S.Sp. (D240) – $1.45

RELIGIONS OF THE WORLD (2 Volumes) – John A. Hardon, S.J. (D241a) – $1.95; (D241b) – $1.45

CHRISTIAN SACRAMENTS AND CHRISTIAN PERSONALITY – Bernard J. Cooke, S.J. (D246) – $1.25

THOUGHTS IN SOLITUDE – Thomas Merton (D247) – $1.25

WE NEUROTICS: A Handbook for the Half-Mad – Bernard Basset, S.J. (D248) – $1.25

NEW TESTAMENT ESSAYS – Raymond E. Brown, S.S. (D251) – $1.45

These prices subject to change without notice

OTHER IMAGE BOOKS

These prices subject to change without notice

OTHER IMAGE BOOKS

MARRIAGE IS FOR GROWNUPS – Joseph and Lois Bird (D291) – $1.75

THE FRIENDSHIP GAME – Andrew M. Greeley (D292) – $1.25

HOW TO BE REALLY WITH IT – Bernard Basset, S.J. (D293) – $1.25

THE ABORTION DECISION – Revised Edition – David Granfield (D294) – $1.45

MEETING GOD IN MAN – Ladislaus Boros, S.J. (D295) – $1.45

A TIME FOR LOVE – Eugene C. Kennedy (D297) – $1.45

CHRIST IS ALIVE! – Michel Quoist (D298) – $1.45

THE MAN IN THE SYCAMORE TREE: The Good Times and Hard Life of Thomas Merton – Edward Rice (D299) – $1.95

THE NEW TESTAMENT OF THE NEW AMERICAN BIBLE (D300) – $1.75

INTRODUCTION TO THE DEVOUT LIFE – Revised Edition – St. Francis de Sales – Translated by Msgr. John K. Ryan (D301) – $1.75

TOWARD A NEW CATHOLIC MORALITY – John Giles Milhaven (D302) – $1.45

THE POWER AND THE WISDOM – John L. McKenzie (D303) – $1.95

INFALLIBLE? AN INQUIRY – Hans Küng (D304) – $1.45

THE DECLINE AND FALL OF RADICAL CATHOLICISM – James Hitchcock (D305) – $1.25

IN THE SPIRIT, IN THE FLESH – Eugene C. Kennedy (D306) – $1.45

THE THIRD PEACOCK – Robert Farrar Capon (D307) – $1.25

THE GOD OF SPACE AND TIME – Bernard J. Cooke (D308) – $1.45

AN AQUINAS READER (Image Original) – Edited with an Intro. by Mary T. Clark (D309) – $2.45

CHRISTIANITY IN THE TWENTIETH CENTURY – John A. Hardon (D310) – $2.45

THE OLD TESTAMENT OF THE JERUSALEM BIBLE – Reader's Edition – Alexander Jones, General Editor
  Volume 1: Genesis – Ruth (D311) – $1.95
  Volume 2: 1 Samuel – 2 Maccabees (D312) – $1.95
  Volume 3: Job – Ecclesiasticus (D313) – $1.95
  Volume 4: The Prophets – Malachi (D314) – $1.95

CHRISTIAN COMMUNITY: Response to Reality – Bernard J. Cooke (D315) – $1.45

THE JESUS MYTH – Andrew M. Greeley (D316) – $1.45

THE SURVIVAL OF DOGMA – Avery Dulles, S.J. (D317) – $1.75

LIVING IN HOPE – Ladislaus Boros, S.J. (D318) – $1.45

These prices subject to change without notice

OTHER IMAGE BOOKS

LOVE IS ALL – Joseph and Lois Bird (D319) – $1.45

THE SOUL AFIRE: Revelations of the Mystics – Ed. by H. A. Reinhold (D320) – $2.45

CONTEMPLATION IN A WORLD OF ACTION – Thomas Merton (D321) – $2.45

AN AUGUSTINE READER (An Image Original) – Edited with an Intro. by John J. O'Meara (D322) – $2.45

HOPE IS THE REMEDY – Bernard Häring, C.Ss.R. (D323) – $1.25

SEX: THOUGHTS FOR CONTEMPORARY CHRISTIANS – Edited by Michael J. Taylor, S.J. (D324) – $1.45

THE CLOUD OF UNKNOWING (and THE BOOK OF PRIVY COUNSELING) – Newly edited with an Intro. by William Johnston, S.J. (D325) – $1.45

WE ARE FUTURE – Ladislaus Boros, S.J. (D326) – $1.45

LET'S START PRAYING AGAIN – Bernard Basset, S.J. (D327) – $1.45

THE NEW SEXUALITY: Myths, Fables and Hang-ups – Eugene C. Kennedy (D328) – $1.45

THE PAIN OF BEING HUMAN – Eugene C. Kennedy (D329) – $1.75

POWER TO THE PARENTS! – Joseph and Lois Bird (D330) – $1.45

A HARSH AND DREADFUL LOVE – William D. Miller (D331) – $1.95

CATHOLIC AMERICA – John Cogley (D332) – $1.75

TO LIVE IS TO LOVE – Ernesto Cardenal (D333) – $1.45

PROTESTANTISM – Martin E. Marty (D334) – $2.45

THE SUPPER OF THE LAMB – Robert Farrar Capon (D335) – $1.75

JOY – Louis Evely (D336) – $1.45

SUFFERING – Louis Evely (D337) – $1.45

OUR PRAYER – Louis Evely (D338) – $1.45

A RELIGION FOR OUR TIME – Louis Evely (D339) – $1.45

IN HIS PRESENCE – Louis Evely (D340) – $1.45

A THOMAS MERTON READER – Revised Edition – Ed. by Thomas P. McDonnell (D341) – $2.95

THE MYSTERY OF SUFFERING AND DEATH – Edited by Michael J. Taylor, S.J. (D342) – $1.75

FIVE FOR SORROW TEN FOR JOY – J. Neville Ward (D343) – $1.45

SAINT-WATCHING – Phyllis McGinley (D344) – $1.75

THOMAS MERTON ON PRAYER – John J. Higgins (D345) – $1.75

LOVE YOUR NEIGHBOR – Louis Evely (D346) – $1.45

WE ARE ALL BROTHERS – Louis Evely (D347) – $1.45

IN THE CHRISTIAN SPIRIT – Louis Evely (D348) – $1.45

ABANDONMENT TO DIVINE PROVIDENCE – Jean-Pierre de Caussade. Trans. by John Beevers (D349) – $1.45

THE SINAI MYTH – Andrew M. Greeley (D350) – $1.75

These prices subject to change without notice

A 75 – 6